INTENTIONAL HR

INTENTIONAL HR

A REVOLUTION IN STRATEGIC THINKING

BY MALLORY HERRIN, SPHR, SHRM-CP, CPLC

NEW DEGREE PRESS

COPYRIGHT © 2021 MALLORY HERRIN

All rights reserved.

INTENTIONAL HR

A Revolution in Strategic Thinking

ISBN	978-1-63730-718-2	*Paperback*
	978-1-63730-855-4	*Kindle Ebook*
	978-1-63730-999-5	*Ebook*

For Jenna and Nathan, my constant inspiration and my reason for everything. I love you both to the moon and back.

Table of Contents

INTRODUCTION		9

PART 1. **IS HR STRATEGIC?** **17**
CHAPTER 1. SETTING UP FOR SUCCESS 19
CHAPTER 2. BEGINNING THE STRATEGIC SHIFT 31
CHAPTER 3. ARE WE THERE YET? 43
CHAPTER 4. MAKING THE CONNECTION 57
CHAPTER 5. EXPLORING THE WHY 69

PART 2. **HR STRATEGY IS MORE CRITICAL TODAY THAN EVER BEFORE** **85**
CHAPTER 6. PEOPLE CENTRICITY 87
CHAPTER 7. THE HUMAN IN HUMAN RESOURCES 103
CHAPTER 8. WHAT WORKERS WANT 119

PART 3. **FINDING SOLUTIONS** **135**
CHAPTER 9. THE RIGHT FOCUS AND MINDSET 137
CHAPTER 10. OVERCOMING THE SKILLS GAP 153
CHAPTER 11. A DIFFERENT APPROACH 165

CONCLUSION 179
ACKNOWLEDGMENTS 185
APPENDIX 189

Introduction

Intentional
adjective
Merriam-Webster definition of *intentional:*
1 : done by intention or design: intended

Revolution
noun
Merriam-Webster definition of *revolution:*
2a : a sudden, radical, or complete change

Human Resource professionals have heard it time and again for over twenty years now: HR needs to be strategic! This means they have to be future-oriented and able to use trends, data, personal knowledge, and expertise to create strategies that achieve goals. While some within human resources *are* strategic in their roles, the vast majority of HR professionals simply are not (even if they think they are). This is due to a variety of factors that may be different for each person, including issues with skill gaps and focusing on the wrong things.

I used to be part of the problem myself, and earlier in my nearly twenty-year long HR career, I wasn't the strategic thinker I am today. Through experience, amazing mentors, shifting my focus and mindset, and upskilling myself, I've changed. Now I'm a successful business leader, strategic partner, and HR consultant. I hold the SPHR and SHRM-CP certifications, and I've spoken throughout the United States at HR conferences, leadership retreats, and in training sessions on topics including HR compliance, leadership, management skills, and more. I've been featured as an HR expert and "industry thought leader" on multiple podcasts, including *HR Insider*. I've served as a fractional HR VP and CHRO for clients, and I've built my own successful HR consulting company, HerrinHR.

I'm not alone in my experience of making this transition. Even the best and brightest in this field have struggled with being a true strategic business partner. Take Johnny C. Taylor, Jr. for example. He's currently the President and CEO of SHRM, the Society for Human Resource Management, which of course is *the* human resources industry association. I had the pleasure of speaking with him and he graciously told me the story of a defining moment in his career that really catapulted him to becoming the strategic business partner that HR leaders aim to become.

The year was 1998, and Johnny was excelling in his early HR career. He led a team of HR professionals that consistently cranked out quality deliverables. Unsurprisingly, he was able to build a world-class HR function for his organization. However, his executive team didn't value it. All of us HR rock stars know the struggle is real, so it's easy to imagine how defeated Johnny and his team might have felt to have worked so hard and so brilliantly, only to find out the work was meaningless to their leadership team.

The problem Johnny had is one many HR practitioners face today. The initiatives he led his team on were important to building a solid HR shop, and he did make some amazing strides with his work in HR for his organization. However, his initiatives weren't all connected to the overall business strategies the executive team were focused on.

He shared with me how he was able to turn this around, and I'll share that with you later in the book. After speaking with Johnny about his experience, I wondered if his story was unique. He was a successful HR leader in a supportive function before making the mental transition to thinking not only about HR, but about business strategy as well. This allowed him to accelerate ahead in both his abilities at the organization he worked for and his career within HR. I reflected on my own career and set out to find how the most effective HR professionals made that leap to a strategic business partner. I'm excited to share I've learned this is something any HR professional can do.

Despite hearing how HR *must* be a strategic partner and understanding how critical HR is to any successful business, a simple conversation with business leaders or other HR professionals reveals HR still isn't quite there yet.

It's no secret business leaders believe there are significant skill gaps in HR professionals' strategic thinking abilities, business acumen, and understanding and use of data and metrics.

CEOs haven't always been happy with HR, but they have been called to action. Alan Guarino, Vice Chairman in Korn Ferry's CEO and Board Services practice, wrote in a 2018 white paper that, "CEOs must take action on something they have never seen done before: they must make HR strategic." In the white paper, Guarino writes that he believes HR is "at the dawn of an enormous transition," as the HR model and department must evolve from an administrative function to a strategic one. He argues if HR is strategic, it will create "breakout performance" and a competitive advantage. I agree with Guarino and second his notion of this transition.

In addition to this call to action for CEOs, I believe many truly *want* HR to rise to the occasion and be the strategic partner they know is so crucial. The proverbial seat at the table, where the big dogs make all the decisions, is just *waiting* for HR. The seat is saved, and it's up to us in HR to get our butts in that seat and show we have the understanding, knowledge, and skills to *stay* in that seat. We owe it to ourselves as HR professionals and to the organizations we serve.

HR is responsible for the people within an organization, which is undoubtedly the most important aspect of a business and has monumental impacts to the bottom line. Gallup's 2017 *State of the American Workplace* report and the book *The Employee Experience Advantage* by Jacob Morgan both clearly illustrate that when a company has a strong HR foundation and is strategic in the right way, the company's performance soars. Businesses have four times higher profit per employee, three times higher revenue per employee, four times the average profit, two times the average revenue, and two times the employee growth.

Don't we all want that kind of success for our employees and our organizations? Don't we want to be the leaders who really *get it* and have the capability to push plans forward and meet the strategic vision of our businesses?

I think we do, and I think it's time to act now. The way in which many people work has changed, largely due to the COVID-19 pandemic. Social unrest has more organizations rightly focused on building better equity and inclusion practices. We are experiencing a talent shortage that is only going to get worse. These are all challenges that must be addressed through HR strategy, in addition to other daily responsibilities HR practitioners face.

I know many people in HR think being truly strategic is hard, but I'm challenging that and I'm challenging *you*.

We need a revolution, and it's here. It's time to stop talking about *how* HR must be a strategic partner and for HR to start *being* a strategic partner. We must be more intentional about the HR function and what we bring to our organizations. We must think and act far beyond the daily administrative activities that are required in our roles. We must be more intentional in our thinking, our HR strategies, our company culture, and how we set employees up for success. We are embarking on a revolution in strategic thinking within HR, and HR professionals must join in—or get left behind in the dust.

If you're intentional in your strategies, if you use the right frameworks, and if you have the right mindset and focus, it is much easier to become a true strategic business partner within HR. Being a true strategic partner bolsters the strategies you create, and frankly, they become much more effective.

When speaking with other HR professionals in my network, I hear the same frustration expressed through often repeated questions: How can I become strategic? How can I be seen as a strategic partner? How can I get a seat at the table?

In my volunteer work, I serve as a mentor to college women pursuing HR through the organization Advanxing Women, and I'm currently on the Student Engagement Committee with DallasHR. These same questions come up with college students, and I feel it is imperative to send them the message HR as we knew it before is dead. It's no longer just an administrative function.

I wanted to write this book because I believe in the power of what we do in HR, and I believe in my fellow HR professionals. I know if I could make the change and become a strategic partner, so too can others.

In this book, I'll share with you my own personal journey in strategic thinking, my failures (and believe me, there have been plenty), what I've learned, and the insights I've gained through loads of research and inspiring conversations. You will hear from amazing business experts and HR leaders from a variety of industries and backgrounds, including Lee Cockerell, Fabia Bourda, Bruce Waller, Johnny C. Taylor, Jr., and more within these pages.

If you're a business owner or executive outside of HR and you want to learn more about what the HR function is all about, and what it can do for your organization when it's given that seat at the table, this book is for you.

If you're a student interested in a career in HR, and you want to know how the HR department is evolving into a must-have strategic function, this book is for you.

Finally, if you're an HR professional hungry for that seat at the table and you want to know how to get it and how to keep it, keep reading. This book has been written for you, with you in mind, so you can learn how to be a valued strategic thinking, business-leading badass.

Join me in this strategic thinking revolution. Make your HR practice more *intentional*.

PART 1

IS HR STRATEGIC?

CHAPTER 1

Setting up for Success

"The secret to getting ahead is getting started."

—MARK TWAIN

Strategic thinking in HR: Is it dead? Did it ever exist in the first place? Is "strategic thinking" nothing more than a mere buzz phrase, thrown around *all the time*, to the point it has been rendered meaningless? What does strategic thinking even mean, and what does it mean within the HR function? Does anyone even care? *Do I even care?*

If you've picked up this book, these may be questions you're asking yourself right now (hopefully not out loud in a crowded workspace—people may think you're having an existential crisis or questioning your career choice if you're an HR professional). Don't worry, though, we're going to answer those questions throughout this book. I'll even go ahead and give a few answers right now. Strategic thinking in HR is *not* dead, it does exist, it is not a myth, and it's not just a buzz phrase (though it may be a little overused).

Strategic thinking in HR and strategies that address the *people* in your organization are essential.

As an HR consultant, I work primarily with small to midsize businesses that often don't have an internal HR representative, let alone an entire HR team. Occasionally, depending on their size, these clients will have someone in HR internally, and of course, I work with their internal HR teams very well when that's the case. However, most of the time, a client will seek out an HR consultant because they don't have anyone and/or there is some kind of "people issue" within the business.

Sometimes it's a toxic workplace environment where people are gossiping left and right. Sometimes employees aren't adhering to time and attendance policies; they may be coming in late or calling out not in accordance with procedure, and it's causing issues with production and scheduling. Sometimes the company might have a rogue manager who just does whatever they want to do (going against what they've been directed to) and leaders are having trouble reeling them in. These, and many other employee issues, can leave leaders wondering how to have uncomfortable, difficult conversations with their teams to rectify the situation.

These business owners and leaders are seeking out an HR consultant because they're experiencing an issue. They know the issue is costing them money, so they are now willing to invest in some HR help to stop the bleeding. The issues affecting the bottom line often result in a lack of productivity and an increase in turnover.

While I absolutely love working with my clients and I am happy to come in and save the day, I also truly believe if you can set up a foundation to be successful from an HR standpoint, you can avoid a lot of these issues to begin with. Businesses must start thinking about investing in HR help, either internally or externally, from a consultant *before* they have ten, fifteen, or twenty employees. It is critical to start thinking about organizational growth—where you want the company to be and what it's going to take to get there. That's just good business.

When it comes to putting together a business plan, the *people* in the organization play a huge role in seeing these plans come to fruition.

Therefore, it behooves us to go ahead and implement HR strategies and get that HR foundation set up from the very beginning, so your growth is supported, on track, and unhindered. The alternative leaves you scrambling to do it later when time is of the essence but you can't focus on the future because the business is bogged down with issues.

Think about those performance standards you want and how you're going to measure performance from the very beginning. It doesn't benefit you to wait to measure performance until you've got twenty-five people on the team. What about the first twenty-four employees? Can they do whatever they want? Does their performance mean nothing? No, their performance matters too, and you don't want to wait to hold them accountable for meeting performance standards.

How about the frequently dreaded creation of your employee handbook and job descriptions? (Seriously, does anyone really *love* writing these things?) These are tactical tasks, but they tie back to your HR strategy.

TACTICAL TASKS SUPPORT STRATEGY
When you're talking about how to measure employee performance, you need to have a job description that clearly outlines essential functions, or job duties, for each position. How can you accurately measure how well an employee is completing their job duties if you don't have a clear understanding of them? Without a clear understanding, not only can you not accurately measure how well an employee is completing their job duties, but your employee may not understand what they are supposed to be doing either. If you want them to knock their work out of the park, they need a solid job description that outlines the essential duties of their role.

To design the positions within your organization, and subsequently create those accurate job descriptions, you must first have clarity on your mission, vision, and values. All of the work performed in your organization needs to support achieving your mission and vision. The way in which work is performed must be aligned with your values. It's important to measure performance with this in mind so you are measuring and evaluating the right things. You wouldn't want to place a high emphasis on meeting production quotas if it encourages employees to cut corners in quality or safety, would you? Of course not!

This also speaks to your company culture. In a nutshell, company culture is "the way things are done around here." It's the culmination of what's valued and rewarded, the environment, interactions between leadership and other employees, as well as the customers. Culture should be intentionally designed, refined, and promoted from day one, and your culture should also be aligned with your mission, vision, and values. If you don't intentionally develop your company culture and work to sustain it, it's going to naturally develop and evolve on its own. A company culture that develops without intentional shaping and continued guidance can easily become toxic. Culture trickles into everything, not just performance. Therefore, your employee handbook also needs to include policies that work to reflect and cultivate your desired company culture.

Summer Jelinek, a leadership development guru, keynote speaker, workshop trainer, and talent coach, spoke with me on this topic. She has worked at some really phenomenal, well-regarded companies, including Disney and HEB, and shared that these organizations understand the importance of HR strategies derived from clarity in the organization's mission, vision, and values. Summer said, "When you're looking at people strategy, you have to understand who you are and where you want to go. [You must ask yourself], 'What decision are we going to make today that aligns with our values to ensure we survive in the future?' If you don't know that starting point, you're just going with the crowd; you're not going to stand out. When I look at companies that are getting it right, it's those companies that know absolutely, without a doubt in their core, who they are."

Let's take this a step further and look at recruiting strategies, which is something every business that plans to hire employees should have, even if you don't have an HR team. What is it going to look like for a candidate? What will the process and experience be for a candidate from A to Z? From the moment you realize you need to hire someone, to making an offer and bringing them on board, this needs to be designed in a way that promotes your culture and values.

Highly successful organizations are intentional in their talent acquisition strategies, as they know how critical it is to get the right people in the right jobs. You will be making an impression as a business throughout the entire recruiting process. You will make impressions with:

Hiring Managers:

- How easy is the process for them?
- Can the process be trusted to get them the right people at the right time?

Your Potential Workforce:

- How easy is it for candidates to apply?
- Do job postings (typically crafted using job descriptions) provide a realistic depiction of what the job entails?
- Does the interview process drag on longer than necessary?
- Does the overall applicant experience reflect your culture and values?

Of course, you want that experience of an applicant going through the recruiting process, the onboarding process, and the orientation to be smooth and an accurate representation of how your organization operates. This even includes considerations of what some may consider minute details. How does the applicant get their information to you as a new hire? Is it a paper process or are you using technology? How user-friendly is it? If it is something they're doing remotely, are you able to communicate in a positive and efficient way? You've got to have those processes defined because it all ties back to the culture you want to build and your company values.

Culture must be aligned with company values, and your company values are a common thread that should be present in all HR strategies. If you want to have a people-centric culture or a service-first culture, make sure you are reflecting that in your recruiting and onboarding processes, your performance management, and everything else.

GET INTENTIONAL FROM THE START

So, while I have touched on a few tactical items, they all tie back to strategic initiatives, and I strongly believe it is important to think about these things and have them in place *before* you need them. It is far better for an organization to think to the future in a proactive manner than to react and scramble. Being proactive and planning your HR strategies is being intentional in HR. Being intentional allows you more control over the result and helps guide you along the way to bring about the result you want.

Let's say you hold off on creating your recruiting strategy and designing that process. If you suddenly find yourself with a hot new contract for your products or services and now you've got to hire a ton of new people, you'll end up with a choppy process that takes up much more of your time than it should. You may also lose good candidates by putting them through your suddenly slapped together process. Even worse, without putting proactive thought into your talent pipeline, you may not even find the best candidates because you're looking in all the wrong places. If you are intentional in HR and create your recruiting strategy and process before it becomes urgent, you can be better prepared for that hot new contract.

You need to build your HR foundation from the beginning. This includes creating your people strategies, designing your processes and procedures, and developing your handbook and job descriptions. Remember, these tactical, administrative tasks are important, as they support strategies.

When I'm meeting with consulting client prospects, sometimes they say to me, "I know I need this. I don't have HR help, but I know it's important. However, we're just too small." HR doesn't become a priority until they hit an arbitrary number of staff members, which varies from person to person, and I've heard all sorts of numbers throughout the years. There is this idea that there is a magic number at which it makes sense to have HR help, and that prior to that number, you don't need it.

As you can see from what I've described above, that's just simply not the case.

The people (employees) have to support where the organization is going. They're in the weeds doing the work and you need to have strategies that are going to ensure everyone's on the same page. They need to understand what they're doing, have the tools to succeed, and be able to perform well to get your business where you want it to go.

You've also got to have strategies that address what's going on in the market, in your external environment, and what's coming in the future. Today, recruiting might not be a huge issue for your business, but if you want to grow from thirty to one hundred employees in a year, then you've got to put together some strategies that will allow that to happen smoothly and address any challenges you may face.

What happens when there is a talent shortage in your industry, and you need highly specialized people to complete your jobs? If that's the case, what sourcing vehicles are you going to use to get a good talent pipeline created? Should you look to colleges and tap into their soon-to-be graduate pool? Do you perhaps need to create an internship program? You don't want to get to the point where you need the bodies in the seat now, but you don't know where to get them because you haven't thought about where to find them proactively.

Or maybe the issue is competition. You don't want to be in a situation where you can't compete with other employers to get the talent on your team because your competitors are offering better pay, better benefits, and/or better advancement and development opportunities. You have to know what your total rewards strategy is going to be, and it needs to be designed *before* you bring people onto your workforce, so you can use it as a tool to attract talent, instead of using it as a retention tool only. Your total rewards strategy should be continuously reviewed and redesigned as needed so you are able to remain competitive with other employers.

If you're not proactively thinking of these things, taking them on, and getting them handled from the very beginning, it can cause huge issues down the road. I see this often, especially when a business owner says, "Oh, I don't need HR help until I've got a lot more employees." I can see where these businesses aren't growing as fast as they want to. They don't have the top talent needed to get the business to the next level, and they have a lot of problems with their workforce in terms of performance and productivity. These challenges absolutely have an impact to their bottom line, and they are struggling.

This could be avoided by setting up that foundation and getting strategic thinking in HR in place from the very beginning.

If this is a lightbulb moment for you, you aren't alone. I didn't always understand the importance of people strategies, and I didn't always think strategically. Truth be told, in the beginning of my HR career, I didn't even understand what that meant. I worked in HR departments completing tactical roles. While the administrative aspects HR professionals are responsible for are important, I didn't feel like I was making a very big difference for any of the employees I served in the organizations I worked in.

I wanted to progress in my field.

I wondered, *are there **any** roles within the HR department I can take on that can truly make a difference? How does HR make a difference? Are there positions I can land where I am doing more than processing FMLA leave requests, answering benefits and payroll questions, etc.?* I was excited to take on a career in HR, but I wanted *more*. It wasn't enough for me to be a paper-pusher. I knew I was too green to be a director or executive making the big decisions, but I wanted to make a real positive impact in the workplace and in people's lives.

Even though it was nerve-wracking, I asked my manager at the time what I could do to get myself to the next level. My boss was very open with me and told me I had potential to move up the ladder, but I needed to work on business acumen. At first, I was a little offended. I had business acumen! I understood how the business worked! However, she was right. Up to that point, I had focused solely on completing my task-based work, but I had never given any thought about how it really fit into the big picture or how what we were doing affected the business overall. Improving my business acumen would help me to see that, as I would have a better understanding of how the business operated, our risks and opportunities, and how everything resulted in some impact to our bottom line.

This would ultimately be what I needed to make any forward movement and get to the next level.

So, I set out on a mission to improve my business acumen and advance myself in my profession and career. I researched what I could on my own, reading business books for as long as I could take it. This was the beginning of my journey to make my work in HR *intentional*. Now is your chance to take control and make your work in HR intentional too. You can start by applying this concept of setting up for success early and proactively in regard to your own career development, as well as your organization's HR function.

CHAPTER 2

Beginning the Strategic Shift

"The ground beneath you is shifting, and either you get sucked in by holding on to old ways, or you take a giant step forward by taking some risks and seeing what happens."

—BONNIE HAMMER

I've always been one of those ambitious go-getter types. I like to really dig into a topic and find out as much as I can about it. In fact, "Learner" is my top strength in Gallup's Strengths-Finder (now CliftonStrengths) assessment. Rounding out my top five strengths are Relator, Strategic (what a shock), Achiever, and Input. Once I realize I don't *really* understand something regarding my work, I'm relentless in my pursuit of knowledge to obtain the understanding I lack. I've never been a "know-it-all" (and honestly, I'm not a fan of people who are), but realizing there was more to the HR profession admittedly made me a little embarrassed.

Around the same time I began devouring any material I could get my hands on to improve my business acumen, I was offered a new HR position at another manufacturing company. This one would provide me with a broader scope of work and I felt this would help me to improve my knowledge and gain more experience. I was thrilled and took the role, but again, I found myself relegated to administrative, tactical functions.

Something had to change if I was going to make a difference and climb the corporate ladder, and I knew it was my responsibility. I decided a great way to make some progress was to earn my Professional in Human Resources (PHR) certification from the Human Resources Certification Institute (HRCI). According to HRCI's website, earning this certification "demonstrates [the credential holder's] mastery of the technical and operational aspects of HR management…"

I took a course to prepare for the exam and during my PHR prep course, I learned more about specific roles within HR and the structuring of HR departments using different models. That was where I learned about the Human Resources Business Partner (HRBP) model. The HRBP is a role that supports a particular division, location, department, etc. and ensures alignment with employees and business objectives in all areas of the HR function.

I realized I had seen this before in job postings online and in articles from the Society for Human Resource Management (SHRM). However, I hadn't taken a dive into what that role really was, as I hadn't always been on the lookout for a new position, and at the time, I wasn't yet a SHRM member.

Once I reviewed a job description for an HRBP, things started clicking into place. There *was* a role where you could make an impact and do more than administrative work at a level below a director. This was it! I was slowly beginning to understand the difference in *tactical* HR work and the *strategic* nature of HR.

At the same time, my own organization was transitioning to using the model of HRBP positions instead of having one HR team that supported the entire organization. This was a model that came about much earlier but was finally gaining more traction because it worked. It turns out strategic thinking in HR really does make a *big* difference for a business, for the better.

So how did it come about?

THE STRATEGIC SHIFT IN HR

In the early 1990s, an influential paper was written by Jay Barney titled "Firm Resources and Sustained Competitive Advantage." This paper, and previous research, spoke of how intangibles, such as the knowledge and skills of employees and an organization's culture, are a big piece of the puzzle in building a business's competitive advantage. This meant the intangibles the HR function had responsibility for had an impact on a business's ability to thrive in the market.

Then, in 1995 Mark Huselid published his study, "The Impact of Human Resource Management Practices on Turnover, Productivity, and Corporate Financial Performance." This study demonstrated how HR practices have a significant impact on the financial results and performance of a business. This marked a turning point for HR, as there became a larger understanding of how HR really should be a strategic function, not just an administrative one. Sure, this idea wasn't new in 1995, but the true value of HR was highlighted and began to be embraced on a larger scale.

In 1997, Dave Ulrich combined these elements and came up with new HR roles that included the strategic partner in his book, *Human Resource Champions*. The strategic partner role is most closely aligned with the HRBP positions of today. Both the HRBP and the strategic partner role are focused on aligning HR activities with business strategy. Dave's book touched on how the HR team should work with line managers to create positive business outcomes.

Eric Van Camp echoed this in a YouTube video titled "What's the Role of HR in Strategic Thinking," stating, "You are the business partner for the line manager and you are leveraging the line manager. Your focus is not on empathy and relationships." He wasn't saying you are *only* the business partner when you have an HRBP title; he was implying if you are in HR, this is the core of your role.

It may have taken fifteen years for the company I was with at the time to embrace the HRBP model and make this shift, but I was able to see it happen. This transition, along with my certification preparation and independent research, helped me to understand more about the strategic role of HR. I was also able to understand how I might be able to take on a position that was more strategic in nature than what I had been doing thus far, even if it wasn't a specific HRBP role.

That's right, you can be a strategic thinker in HR no matter what your title is. You just need to first understand what it means, and then how to apply it to your work, which didn't happen right away for me.

While I do think some people are naturally strategic thinkers, I wasn't always a strategic thinker when it came to HR. I've always been a worrier and often worked through scenarios in my head, be it personal or in business. I would think of all the worst-case scenarios that could happen and come up with solutions in an effort to avoid them. This kind of worrying is very similar to strategic thinking, in that the worrier anticipates challenges and proactively thinks up solutions to avoid them. However, when it came to HR, I initially didn't carry over my "worry thinking" about the future, and I was part of the problem myself.

Way back in the beginning of my career, I didn't even set out to be a part of the human resources department. It was handed to me when I was in accounting. I soon discovered I really loved HR (a hell of a lot more than I liked accounting), and it has since become my passion. I reasoned being in HR provided a better chance than accounting work did to make a difference in the lives of the individuals employed within an organization. This really resonated with me as I'm naturally empathetic and big on helping others whenever I can. At the time, I decided HR was what I wanted to pursue as a career, but of course, I also knew I had a lot to learn.

I took on roles that would allow me to improve my skills and learn more about the various functions in HR such as recruiting, benefits, compensation, employee relations, training and development, HRIS systems, etc. You name it, I wanted to know about it. Although I wanted to find a way to help people through HR, I wanted to progress in my career and was more heavily focused on that at the time. I wanted to get promotions and move up the ladder and be the best in my field.

I didn't realize I was starting to build my strategic thinking brain within HR.

SEEING THE BIG PICTURE

As I took on roles that submersed me in different functional areas within HR, I was starting to see how all the different pieces fit together—but I was still missing one key element. I was missing knowledge of the bigger picture: how the administrative, tactical work in HR ties into the company's strategic objectives overall.

For example, earlier in my career, one of my main job duties was processing Family and Medical Leave Act (FMLA) leave requests. I kicked ass with this task. I processed the requests quickly and I had the entire process nailed down. I knew the FMLA inside and out. My focus when processing FMLA requests was primarily on what was legally required of the company. Second to that, I aimed to make the request process a pleasant one for employees already faced with a challenging personal situation.

I didn't understand FMLA leave was just one small part of our total rewards strategy and that our total rewards strategy was a larger part of our attraction and retention initiatives.

The way I saw it, we offered FMLA because we had to by law. What I didn't understand was why we had designed other leave of absence options that mirrored FMLA for those who weren't FMLA eligible. This "other" leave was a part of our total benefits package. This way, the company was doing more than was legally required to treat all employees fairly and offer an appealing benefit to attract and retain talent. This other leave was a way for the company to say, "Hey, everyone, come work here! You can still take a leave of absence even if you don't meet FMLA requirements! That's how much we care!"

I wanted to understand the bigger picture, so I found myself in my boss's office asking, "Why?" Having a conversation with my managers about this and asking why we had these other leave types when we were only *required* to have FMLA helped me build an understanding of strategy. It started clicking for me when I started asking questions about why these things were so critical beyond a compliance standpoint.

Other pivotal moments that helped to shift my strategic thinking included more questioning about the "why."

I remember one boss I had was particularly tough on me when I was working in compensation. I'd be assigned a task and would promptly return it to her completed. She'd then send it right back to me and say, "You need to make sure you have the right headers and footers, the title panes should be frozen in this Excel spreadsheet, and this needs to be formatted to print." Ahem, excuse me? Was the formatting really the point of the task? I just thought she was being incredibly picky, and because she was relentless in her criticism of what I didn't consider important, I also thought she must hate me.

I went to her one day and asked her why this stuff mattered when the content of what I was turning in was accurate and on time. I expected her response to be negative and directed at me personally, but she explained to me something that has stuck with me ever since.

She asked me to keep perspective.

Our leaders would be using the deliverables to make important decisions about the future of our business. We wanted what we produced within HR to be organized, accurate, and impressive. She told me to think about who's going to see these reports in our finance and operations departments. "How will they see you if you consistently turn in deliverables that they know will be accurate and ready to use, versus if you consistently turn in deliverables they need to adjust the format on just to do something as simple as printing it out?"

While the information of my reports and the tasks I had completed were accurate, even the headers and footers were important. We needed to show we took this seriously and the deliverables we gave were going to be exceptionally high quality every single time.

It's not always easy for leaders to really give a voice to HR. One of the best ways we are able to gain support and buy in for the initiatives we want to implement in HR is through consistency, quality, and tying things back to the bottom line. What we were doing in the compensation department was exactly that. That was where I was able to start seeing the bigger picture and how even little things mattered within that bigger picture.

I started pushing myself from that moment on to give the highest quality deliverables I could. As minute as this seems, it sparked my interest in understanding the rest of our business too. What kind of decisions were made based on the information in the deliverables? How did they affect the business and the employees? (Look at that—the beginnings of strategic thinking!)

I started meeting with department heads outside of HR because I wanted to know more about their responsibilities and functions, and how everything tied in together. I was soaking up as much knowledge as I possibly could to understand how everything connected and how the information I was producing would be used. I'm grateful for the knowledge that was shared with me, as it gave me a broader understanding. I learned how everything worked together and how the role of HR affected all of the other departments in the entire business. There were people in every other department, after all, and what does HR concern itself with? The people.

One of the department leaders I met with, whose brain I was picking, gave me an exercise. He told me it might be a good idea to do a SWOT analysis to help me think about the business as a whole. This is where you assess a company's strengths, weaknesses, opportunities, and threats. I did because this would help me learn more about the business and the challenges we faced. It wasn't exactly what I would call fun at first. In fact, I felt it was overwhelming and a torturous form of "homework," but *wow*, did it open my eyes.

When I started expanding my area of focus onto the business overall, it helped me to start thinking in a proactive way from the HR perspective. I thought about how we could prepare for challenges and either prevent or address them. This really shifted my thinking quite a bit.

After that job, I had much more knowledge under my belt, my first HR certification (outside of payroll), and by the time I left that position, my boss had told me she could really see how I was able to think in a full circle. I could now see how everything was correlated and how all the puzzle pieces in the business fit together. This led me to anticipate what someone's questions might be when we designed something as simple as a new paid time off request process. I could understand how something we did in HR was going to affect a team and how it was going to impact even an individual employee. When I made a presentation, I could give all of that information in advance, and I could point out blind spots to my team when we were developing something.

After asking why, and learning more about the role of HR and the business as a whole, I was finally applying strategic thinking within HR. I made it a habit to think through the entire scenario, anticipate problems, and proactively come up with solutions.

I had finally joined the strategic thinking revolution, and if I can do it, anyone can. The HRBP model has been around for more than just a hot minute by now. Even if you aren't in a position with an HRBP, director, or executive title, you too can begin your own strategic shift, and there's no better time than the present to do it.

CHAPTER 3

Are We There Yet?

"Nothing has such power to broaden the mind as the ability to investigate systematically and truly all that comes under thy observation in life."

—MARCUS AURELIUS

Ah, human resources management, my beloved profession. The heart of a company, the wind in the sails of top organizations, and the "strategic approach to effective management of people in a company or organization such that they help their business gain a competitive advantage." Big thanks to Phil Johnson, author of *Human Resources Management: A Critical Approach*, for that definition; it ruins the poetic bravado I was going for, but it really hits the nail on the head. More succinctly stated in another book on HR management, it's the "process of employing people, training them, compensating them, and developing strategies to retain them" (*Human Resource Management*, 2016).

Human resources is a critical business function centered around the most important aspect of a business: the people.

A BRIEF HISTORY OF HR

Human resources management is just as described in the definition above: strategic. It may be shocking to some, but it didn't start that way. Sandra Reed's definitive book, *PHR and SPHR Professional in Human Resources Certification Complete Study Guide*, provides a fantastic summary of the evolution of the HR profession. (This is also a book I would highly recommend to anyone studying to obtain their own HR certifications.) Reed wrote that at the end of the nineteenth century, the Industrial Revolution brought about a major change in the nature of work. Small businesses, managed by sole proprietors, gave way to larger organizations that required management through specialized functions designed to maximize efficiency and productivity. By the 1920s, the *personnel* department/function (sometimes called industrial relations) was born.

In a LinkedIn article, Vinay Kumar S provided another excellent timeline of the HR function. He wrote the human resources function's roots can be found in the personnel department of yesteryear. Way back in the day, the personnel function was the purely tactical people function, concerned with hiring, training, evaluating, and paying employees. As businesses grew even larger and best practices began to develop within the personnel role, formal training standards were needed and colleges started to offer courses in this field (Reed, 2019).

The article further provided an explanation for the shift to what we think of as "HR" today. By the mid-twentieth century, most businesses had a personnel department, and by the late 1970s, the personnel function began to transform into *human resources management*. This was in response to regulatory complexities in employment law, business globalization, technological advances, and increasing market competition within American business.

Human resources management encompassed the staff functions handled by the *personnel* department previously, but now also included responsibilities in people management. The HR function was starting to take on responsibility for ensuring organizational effectiveness through employee performance.

By the 1990s, human resources management had been proven to have a significant impact on a business' bottom line. As mentioned in Chapter Two, research by Mark Huselid, Jay Barney, and others showed how human resources strategies affected talent acquisition, retention, development, productivity, and more. Then, in the mid-1990s, Dave Ulrich (the father of the modern strategic HR business partner role) redesigned HR positions through his model of HR roles. The heavy push for HR as a strategic function was born, leading to our current definition of human resources management. What a journey!

Knowing the origin story of the HR function and what it is today, you'd think everyone who has ever had a job at any organization would know and understand what HR is and what they do. I've always been curious as someone within HR to know what others think HR is and what they think of HR. Unfortunately, despite the function being around for about a hundred years or more, you'd be surprised at how many people struggle with this.

THE PERCEPTION OF HR

When I'm out and about meeting new people, I'll inevitably be asked what I do for a living. The very moment I say, "I work in HR," I am typically met with a response of, "Oh, so you fire people?" My good friends have even joked about me dressing as the Terminator for Halloween because, yes, discharging employees is a part of the job in HR. This view of HR is pretty narrow, but it's not uncommon.

I recently spoke with Malcolm Louth, Chief Human Resources Officer of PRYM Group, and he shared that this view is something he runs into as well. "Forty years ago, companies needed somebody to [handle] sickness management and wages, and that's what we know to be personnel." Of course, we know the function of HR has changed over time, but we may not be doing our part to help others truly understand the new(er) nature of HR, which contributes to this narrow and inaccurate view of the profession. Malcolm pointed out many of us within HR don't necessarily do a great job of explaining this shift, and I have to say I've been guilty of it myself. "Anyone that's really good in HR, before COVID-19, if you met them in a pub, [they would be] embarrassed…that people don't know what [HR] is. People will say, 'Oh, you do hiring and firing or handle wages.' Most HR people don't want to be the boring person who explains what they do, so they say, 'Yeah, you're right…it's something like that.'"

When Malcolm pointed this out, it really resonated with me. I've had the same encounter countless times, and I haven't done my part to really explain HR. Sure, in the moment, perhaps it saves me from a social faux pas in over explaining what I do, but in the grand scheme of things, all I can say is *oof*. I really should be helping to transition the perception of the profession I'm on fire for. In these moments, if we aren't doing our part to clear up any confusion, we're perpetuating this narrowed view.

Malcolm continued, "In a modern world, HR is the glue to most organizations." He's not wrong. I suggest all of us in HR do our part when faced with this common scenario. When socializing in our personal lives or (especially) when networking, we are each provided with the opportunity to help others see HR in a new light.

Armin Trost, a German psychologist and professor widely regarded as an HR thought leader, illustrates this perception issue in a fantastic video series on strategic HR. Trost asked hundreds of people over the course of fifteen years (all experienced professionals) what they thought about HR. He found their responses were often the same. Employees may say HR is part of the hiring process or that they conduct employee satisfaction surveys every year. Some he asked mentioned HR made their managers conduct performance reviews, even though they didn't think they were very effective and managers didn't want to be bothered with them. Many would say HR was the department you've got to keep happy, as you don't want to have to go to HR. It's as if those in HR were evil high school principals acting as the fun police at work. Watch out, or HR is going to get you!

Very rarely would he get any response about HR being the most important function in any organization. There were no mentions of HR being about people and their creativity, motivation, development, etc. As you can see, HR is sadly misunderstood and still viewed as the personnel department it began as long ago. Even sadder is how executives still sometimes share this old school perception of HR.

I love HR, and I know what HR is capable of, so I want to change that perception and do my part to advance our profession. I am committing to help more people understand what HR really is. If we *all* embrace it as a strategic function and HR leaders as strategic business partners, we can help change the narrative about HR on a wider scale.

EVERYONE HATES HR
Clearly, HR isn't just misunderstood by business leaders. Let's get real here—employees just don't like HR. They don't like the department and often the professionals in it, and we get a bad reputation. Due to this, I typically give a qualifier when I tell someone I work in HR and say, "Oh, but don't worry, I'm the cool HR lady, I'm not the bad guy."

Just like any other professional, I like to stay on top of news and trends in my chosen field. It's not uncommon for me to read articles and blog posts about HR. Sometimes content of this nature is automatically suggested for me as soon as I open Google. I find it as common as ads for toasters that pop up in my social media feeds the very moment I think it might be time for a new one at home.

Occasionally, an article will fall into my lap about how disliked HR is or why HR is irrelevant. This happened not too long ago, as I came across an article by Susan M. Heathfield titled "Reasons Why Employees Hate HR."

I glanced at the title and felt a cocktail of emotions. First, I felt a little outraged. I thought to myself, *employees don't hate HR. If they have a negative feeling toward the function, they likely don't understand it.* I reflected on this a little and continued my inner monologue. *If employees don't hate HR, why do I give the qualifier that I'm actually not the bad guy when I tell someone my profession? I know they don't like HR and I try to stop people from judging me negatively for being an HR professional.*

Then I took a deep breath, stopped being personally offended, and thought, *employees actually may not like HR for completely valid reasons.* These reasons are likely more than a simple lack of understanding the function, and this made me feel a little defeated. Maybe an employee hates HR because they feel like HR kills the vibe, always saying no and enforcing policies. I mean, if a dress code policy doesn't allow for casual wear or fun hair colors, tattoos, or piercings, an employee may feel there is no real business purpose to this. This can lead to an employee feeling they can't express themselves for no good reason whatsoever, and who writes the dress code policy? HR.

Heathfield's article covered much of what I've read in similar articles before and used information gathered from "the observations of readers, managers, and other HR employees who read articles at TheBalanceCareers." Some of the six reasons given for the "hatred" include a belief that those in

HR are dishonest and untrained, as well as employees not understanding what HR really does.

Heathfield also touched on perhaps the biggest complaint from employees when it comes to human resources: HR is focused on the company and their managers, *not* the employees. Heathfield writes, "To some employees, HR seems to care only about the interests of the company and the managers. In any employee complaint situation, HR appears to side with the manager the majority of the time. Even if you have multiple witnesses or employees who have repeatedly complained to HR about the same behavior, HR sides with the company." How many times have I heard HR only cares about the company? I imagine as much as you have—too many times to count.

In a previous job, I worked with both bargained (unionized) and non-bargained employees at a manufacturing company. The non-bargained employees were either fans of HR and appreciative of our efforts, or they largely ignored us. Internal surveys indicated the non-bargained employees generally didn't have a negative perception of the HR department, its work, or its staff.

No survey was necessary to know exactly how the bargained employees felt. They, along with their union reps, were quite vocal about their feelings toward HR, and it wasn't good. They thought we were downright evil, protecting the company at all costs with no regard to the bargained employees, and saying "no" whenever we could just to stick it to them. I'd come into work as the third shift was leaving and the first shifters were coming in for the day. On many occasions, I would arrive and walk in to see a union rep or two yelling at one of the HR managers. Occasionally, they would yell in the general direction of the HR offices about the unfairness of HR's policies and what not.

I made it a personal mission to, one, never be yelled at by a union rep and, two, do what I could to shift this perspective of my team as much as possible. At the same time, I noticed by that point, my colleagues were rather annoyed with the union reps and weren't all that interested in listening to what they had to say. Many of my colleagues and managers certainly didn't want to "go above and beyond" to help them. They had put up a wall (both emotionally and physically in the building) that separated HR from the union reps, and this carried through in all of their interactions. This further alienated the union reps and hindered any kind of positive, open communication. We might as well have put up a big, neon sign that read, "*Go away, we don't want to help you.*"

So, whenever it was my turn to help a union rep out, I would take the time to really listen to them and understand their needs. I'd also take the time to ask them about their day and try to get to know them a little bit as a fellow human being. When I did have to say "no" to a request or deliver news I knew wouldn't go over well, I'd be as transparent as I was allowed to be. I would take care in explaining the reasoning behind the "no" or the bad news. Over time, this combination of empathy, curiosity of my coworker's worlds, and transparent education worked phenomenally. The union reps didn't yell at me. They asked me how my day was going. When I had to tell them "no" and explained why, they accepted it and didn't push back, though they did sometimes have follow-up questions. We were able to work well together, and I actually enjoyed my conversations with these guys!

Unfortunately, their perspective of HR as a whole didn't change much, and they still felt we were primarily the puppets of company executives. At least during my time there, I did my part to start that perspective shift, making it easier for HR and the union reps to work together and communicate.

When speaking with my HR peers, they have confirmed this "us versus them" mentality isn't uncommon. Many also face the view of HR as support for the company and the company alone. However, it doesn't occur solely in union environments.

John Crowley at People HR explored this idea in his blog titled *Are All HR Professionals Incompetent?* His blog stated while there are many reasons employees dislike their HR department's competence level, one reason that comes up more often than others is the belief HR cannot be trusted. Crowley expanded on this, writing, "A common assumption is that HR does not care about staff, and is just an evil extension of the CEO, with a mandate to do all of the unpopular dirty work."

Crowley stated he doesn't think this complaint proves much as it relates to competence levels in HR, but he did conduct a Twitter poll in 2017 that confirmed "more than 50 percent of employees believe their HR department sides with the company over employees." (I mean, it's a Twitter poll so take that for what it's worth, but I can say from personal experience prior to becoming a consultant, this sentiment does ring true for *a lot* of people.)

Cynthia Shapiro, author of *Corporate Confidential*, is a former HR executive who was interviewed by ABC News regarding some of the "dirty little secrets" in HR. Shapiro began her segment by relaying the story of a colleague—an HR director—who would display a photo of two children on her desk, facing the front of her desk. This was intentional, so when the director was interviewing job candidates, the applicants were baited into commenting on the photo and talking about their own children. The HR rep in this instance didn't actually have children but had a directive from upper management not to hire any mothers. She tricked people into disclosing they were parents. (Shady, shady, shady. I do not approve.)

Shapiro went on to state she has also heard of those in HR offering to walk a candidate back to their vehicle following an interview. This seems like a nice gesture, but in actuality, it was designed to take a peek inside a candidate's car to check for baby seats. Further, she went on to say HR professionals are there on behalf of the company and not employees. "That's what people like me were paid the big bucks to do—find the gray areas around the law so the company can do what it wants to do."

I won't deny there are some "leaders" out there working for companies that really don't have employees' best interests at heart. These executives fully expect their HR teams to do exactly what Shapiro said: shut up and let them do what they want.

HR IS NOT A PUPPET

A former client of mine was *not* happy about Section Seven of the Fair Labor Standards Act, which requires employers to provide reasonable breaktime for employees to express breast milk for their nursing child(ren) up to one year following the child(ren)'s birth. This client even directly asked me how they could get around this. They didn't want to allow nursing mothers the breaktime, and they absolutely didn't want to provide a space for the purpose. They were hoping perhaps it would violate a health code and that would get them out of their obligation. When that wasn't the case, the client wanted "creative solutions" from me.

I didn't give them an out. I did provide them with suggestions that would help ease any burden to the business from operational and financial standpoints primarily, but I took a hard stance here. You *must* comply with this, and you will *not* retaliate against anyone who needs this breaktime. You will *not* change your hiring practices to avoid employing nursing mothers either. Yes, it took some education and explanation regarding potential consequences of noncompliance, but I was by no means going to back down and be one of those "puppets for the company."

It's probably easier for me to do that because I'm an outside third party, so my job isn't in jeopardy if I take a hard stance, but those who work internally in HR need to stand up for what's right, too. Easier said than done, I know, but it's our job. If you can't take the heat, maybe HR isn't for you.

If someone in HR is engaging in underhanded behavior, like trying to trick mothers into disclosing they have children during an interview for nefarious purposes, then yes, HR truly *is* acting on behalf of the company. In situations like that example, HR isn't looking out for the interests of employees at all, but this is unprofessional and unacceptable, and this is the exception and not the rule in my experience (as it should be).

Shapiro left the world of HR to assist employees with fighting against their employers. While there are undoubtedly instances where that is exactly what's needed because an employer really may be screwing an employee over, most of us within HR either find a different approach to reach the desired outcome or find another position where we are empowered to do the right thing.

We are tasked with striking that balance of protecting the company, furthering the organization, and watching out for the best interests of employees. It's not always an easy feat, but the good ones get it done, which in turn lessens the perception of HR as "hated" by employees.

The more we can do to shift the general belief of what HR actually does, the better. The evolution of HR over time has led us from the personnel department to HR's strategic role, but it still isn't accepted and viewed as such by nearly enough people. The general public doesn't inherently understand what we do beyond hiring and firing people. Even those within our own organizations see HR as a paper-pushing function that forces activities onto managers and employees that they don't understand or value.

So, while HR as a strategic player in business isn't a new concept, we still aren't really *there* yet. We haven't quite arrived to the party as the key strategic function we should be. We won't get there until there has been a much more massive shift in the perception of HR.

CHAPTER 4

Making the Connection

"First find out what you are capable of, then decide who you are."
—TARA WESTOVER

When it comes to leaders in HR, Johnny C. Taylor, Jr. is by far one of the best, as any HR professional involved in our industry organization (the Society for Human Resource Management, better known as SHRM) can tell you. Johnny has been the President and CEO of SHRM since June of 2017, and his leadership has driven SHRM in its endeavor to advance the HR profession tremendously. He's an attorney, author, columnist for *USA Today*, and an avid public speaker. He's been featured in the media and in publications such as *Time*, *The Wall Street Journal*, and *Fortune* (among others) and has also testified before Congress quite a few times, covering workforce issues such as paid leave and sexual harassment. (Is there anything this man *can't* do?)

I recently spoke with him and was shocked to learn even he has previously struggled with convincing business leaders of the strategic value of HR, and he, too, believes HR practitioners need to become more strategic in both their mindset and work.

CEO EXPECTATIONS AND BRIDGING STRATEGIES
I suppose it shouldn't have come as a shock; after all, there's plenty of data that illustrates this perspective from C-suite HR leaders. Korn Ferry, a well-known consultancy concentrated on human resources, surveyed 189 CHROs throughout the globe on this topic and the results showed 41 percent of CHROs reported business acumen as the skill they most desired to possess, and 28 percent reported their highest need was the ability to turn strategy into action.

Further, Professor Nick Holley of Henley Business School's Centre for HR Excellence compiled research that concluded CEOs wanted to be "good customers of HR…and they do want HR to take a strategic role" but they believed HR didn't deliver. Holley determined C-suite executives wanted HR to play a key strategic role, but those within HR needed to make it happen themselves.

CEOs aren't always going to hand out the keys to the kingdom and provide a seat at the table without HR professionals really showing up. We have to demonstrate our strategic thinking abilities and the value we can bring.

The statistics are alarming. Development Dimensions International, a global leadership consulting firm, teamed with The Conference Board and EY for their 2018 Global Leadership Forecast report. Over twenty-five thousand business leaders and twenty-five hundred HR professionals were surveyed. This research showed only 11 percent of CEOs rated their HR teams' skills as "good" when it came to forecasting company employment needs and linking employee development to business planning. This was a decline from the previous 20 percent that was reported just three years prior.

When I asked Johnny about strategic thinking in HR, he said, "There's a strategy in everything, and the real opportunity for us as HR professionals is to think of strategy within our HR practice, and then strategy of the business that we work in that we service." Basically, we need to build a great HR function, but remember the purpose of the HR function is to help move the needle forward for overall business objectives.

Johnny explained within our HR strategy, we must ensure what we are doing is actually strategic. "So, what HR leaders can do in terms of strategy on the HR side, is to literally think big picture. What's the future of work going to look like; what are some of the macro issues occurring in the larger culture and how are those [issues] impacting how people show up to work every day and how they experience work, and in many instances, why they leave a particular workplace?"

HR strategy, as he defines it, is all about "designing specific interventions to help solve for the big macro people-related issues we now have to deal with in the workplace," as well as "being prepared certainly for today, and getting prepared for tomorrow." This is just one piece of the puzzle. As Johnny mentioned, the other piece is understanding and participating in the strategy of the business.

In an *HR Magazine* article written by Tony Lee and Dana Wilkie, Evan Sinar, Chief Scientist at DDI, is quoted as concluding, "If HR wants to be seen as a strategic business partner in the C-suite, they need to go beyond just carrying out the business needs of today. They need to prove that they are basing their strategy and decisions on solid data, and they need to demonstrate—often using visualization and storytelling techniques—how those decisions are linked to better business results and financial performance."

The business strategy all comes down to exactly that: business results and financial performance. Unfortunately, this is an area I'd mark as "in need of improvement" if we were rating the performance of the HR function and HR practitioners as a whole. Johnny agreed, saying, "From a business perspective, what many of us fail to do is understand the business's strategy, and that's when HR has to partner *with business* to understand. Frankly, a lot of people don't understand the business strategy, [but] they understand the HR strategy, and the two are bridging."

This issue is a huge component of the reason why HR isn't seen as a valuable strategic function to many business leaders outside of HR. When HR isn't a key strategic partner, and is treated as just another administrative function, that naturally gives rise to employees hating HR. Why? Well, HR becomes mostly ineffective at that point in terms of impacting and improving the employee experience. Those in HR must know and understand the *business* strategy to create effective *HR* strategies that support it. If we don't do this, we are perpetuating this perspective of HR as solely administrative.

Sometimes it takes a personal failure to realize this, and even Johnny learned this lesson the hard way.

Johnny C. Taylor, Jr. is one of my own personal HR heroes, and someone I consider to be our nation's HR leader. I nearly couldn't believe it when he told me about his own experience with this early in his career. He had a practice of bringing his HR team together at the beginning of each year to determine the specific strategies and deliverables the team would work on. "We would deliver famously, maniacally on our strategic imperatives. What we failed to do was sit down with the business leaders and ask, 'Do you value any of this?'"

He distinctly remembered in 1998 cranking out all of their HR deliverables and doing a phenomenal job, but at the end of the year, the organization's executives didn't seem to appreciate all of his HR team's hard work. They said to him, "None of this matters to us. What we really wanted you to do was X."

Johnny said, "We had never actually merged HR strategy and the business strategy."

Since then, he's corrected this disconnection between HR strategy and the business strategy. One method he used to bridge the gap was including HR strategies that would drive the business. So, if he had five initiatives for his HR team for the upcoming year, he would make sure three of them would be things the HR team must do to ensure they were a good HR shop. The other two initiatives would be what really mattered to the business leaders.

That isn't necessarily the magic number when it comes to including specific initiatives that matter to business leaders. The point is as an HR professional, you are working on initiatives within your HR function while also including some your business leaders prioritize.

HR professionals must do our part to bridge HR strategy and business strategy together, and that starts with really understanding the business strategy and finding out what our executive teams want from HR. That's what it's going to take to change the perception of HR, especially among our executive teams.

SHOWING UP AS A STRATEGIC PARTNER
Research, such as Professor Holley's study, has shown some CEOs really *get it,* but they need HR to step up to the plate. However, what about those who truly *don't* understand the strategic nature of HR? Perhaps all an executive has experienced with HR has been administrative. This wouldn't be a far-reaching assumption, seeing as how so many business leaders are still hoping for HR to become strategic partners.

Can these executives really be faulted when this has been their experience? On one hand, sure, it stands to reason someone leading a business in any executive capacity would have a pretty good grasp on what other functions can and should *do* in an organization (or at least a general idea). On the other hand, however, HR as a strategic partner in business is still a relatively new concept when you look at the entire history of the function.

HR professionals aren't always able to convince their executives of the strategic value of HR either. As I network with other HR professionals, this frustration comes up time and again. I also encounter it in my own work as a consultant at times, and this is a topic I mentor other HR professionals through as well.

As Evan Sinar pointed out above, HR professionals need to show business leaders we are strategic thinkers, and one great way to do this is through visualization and storytelling. I'm going to further illustrate how HR professionals must bridge HR strategy and business strategy by doing just that. So, grab your popcorn, it's story time!

An HR professional I mentor was once faced with quite a predicament. We'll call her Linda to protect her identity. For a little background, Linda had begun her tenure with her company as an office manager, and over time, she took on more HR responsibilities. After about seven years of working for the company, she was promoted to HR director, though her only HR experience had been within her role as an office manager.

Linda's company was run by its founder for over forty years before he retired thirteen years into Linda's time there. During his reign and after, everything the HR team did was administrative and compliance driven. The company's leadership changed when the founder retired.

Toxicity began brewing within the workforce. Sadly, the toxicity was modeled by the new leadership regime and worsened as the years went by. The new executives began replacing other upper management employees with colleagues they'd worked with before, and while this isn't an unheard-of practice, in this case, it bred resentment from employees who had been loyal to the now replaced directors. On top of that, the new leaders didn't have the best "people skills."

The new leaders ran a tight ship through fear and intimidation. It wasn't uncommon for them to yell at employees, often using profanity. They gossiped about their direct reports' work and personal lives to just about anyone who would listen, upper management or not. They also demanded employees do more with less resources in an already lean organization, resulting in declining work/life balance.

The management practices of the new leadership team began to tank morale. Productivity started to suffer as a result. Linda would update the C-suite on people issues plaguing the company, sharing how employees complained of favoritism, unrealistic performance standards, and general mistreatment. Her concerns would fall on deaf ears or be met with defensive remarks about how people just needed to pull their weight and "quit their bitching."

Then things came to a head for Linda. An employee—let's call him David—confided to Linda he was being harassed due to his sexual orientation. The alleged harasser? One of the new leaders in upper management—we'll call her Sonia. Sonia had begun to repeatedly berate David for "performance issues" (side note—he didn't work in her department) and it seemed to most of the staff she was out to get him.

Sonia's mistreatment of David began when her pet employee, Janice, began blaming David for her own failure to meet deadlines, though records and data proved David didn't have a thing to do with it. Janice consistently used David as a scapegoat, which created tension, and Sonia began to make comments about David all over the office. At first, these comments weren't made to David directly (which is still horrible) and they were in regard to work. "David can't handle his workload. David's sloppy work puts a strain on my team. If David can't get it together, how can we do our jobs?" Over the course of a few weeks, Sonia began making comments to David directly *and* began commenting on him personally. This included comments about his sexual orientation. (I'm going to spare you some quotes here, as they are absolutely appalling.)

Once Linda became aware of the situation when David reported it, she knew she had to do something. She informed the CEO of the complaint and told him she wanted to launch an investigation. He resisted, saying, "It's all high school drama. People are going to gossip and David just needs to get over it." *Yikes.*

My jaw dropped when I heard this. What kind of (pardon my French) bullshit was this? What was wrong with the CEO? With Sonia? Linda asked me for guidance. She desperately wanted to resolve the situation for David and do what she could to protect the company from a potential lawsuit.

I explained to her the CEO needed to fully understand the ramifications of the situation and it was her duty to educate him. He needed to know the compliance issues and legal risks certainly, as well as the short- and long-term effects to their business strategy.

This was a lightbulb moment for Linda. She hadn't thought about how employee issues would impact business strategy. The company's business objectives included aggressive growth in the market and an expansion of their physical footprint, among other initiatives. To achieve those goals, they needed to secure more funding and they planned to increase their staff in the following fiscal year.

Linda was then able to explain to the CEO this sort of complacency regarding the work environment and the decline of their company culture would affect the company's employer brand in a very negative way. Employees who were fed up with the mistreatment and unrealistic standards would begin leaving to work for competitors, and a few had already left. The company's reputation as a terrible place to work would spread, hindering their ability to attract new talent, and that, combined with heavy turnover, would drive a significant drop in productivity and an even heavier decline in revenues. Their business strategies relied on boosting revenue, attracting investors, and increasing their staff—not to mention the damage that would result from a lawsuit if nothing was done regarding David's complaint.

This got the CEO's attention. Linda was then able to take appropriate action with the CEO's support.

This story is a little extreme, but there are lessons to be learned from it. First, Linda was forced to be very reactive to the situation. While we can't always predict employee issues such as what Linda experienced, it is far better to be proactive when it comes to risk mitigation. Being strategic involves being proactive. We must work to anticipate challenges and find ways to prevent them, or to overcome them if prevention isn't possible. Just as Johnny said, we must be prepared for today as well as the future.

For the second lesson, we can build off of being proactive when it comes to strategy. What if Linda had implemented change management initiatives when the new leaders came into the business? How about a plan to fortify company culture? The company didn't have annual sexual harassment training as part of their compliance and risk mitigation initiatives, but could Sonia's treatment of David have been prevented if they did? Knowing the overall business strategy, revisiting or creating new employee retention and talent acquisition programs would have been appropriate. These are just a few examples, but the lesson here is this: if effective HR strategies that built both a solid HR shop *and* positioned the business for success had been put into place, imagine what a difference it would have made.

People, and people issues, greatly affect a company's ability to achieve results. We must be strategic partners with our executives to mitigate risk while at the same time driving the business forward.

CHAPTER 5

Exploring the Why

"All highly competent people continually search for ways to keep learning, growing, and improving. They do that by asking why. After all, the person who knows how will always have a job, but the person who knows why will always be the boss."

—BENJAMIN FRANKLIN

Hopefully by now I've made a clear case, for anyone who didn't already agree, that HR plays an integral role in business strategy. Now that we know there is a problem with HR professionals being key strategic players in their organizations, I want to get to the *why* behind it. Why don't other business professionals and leaders see HR professionals as strategic? What are HR professionals doing and not doing to perpetuate this perspective, what are they missing, and why aren't they driving strategy?

I know for myself, I wasn't always strategic or moving the needle forward for any business objectives through the HR function in the past. As you'll see throughout this book, I've shared that early in my career, I wasn't able to be strategic because I just didn't get it. I, like many others in HR, was reactive in my role and working from a purely tactical place. Even in lower-level positions where I wouldn't be expected to be strategic, I didn't understand how HR practices affected the business in a meaningful way.

It took a change in my perspective, and a lot of learning, before I truly understood how HR is a strategic function. It also took a lot of professional development on my part. In particular, I needed better business acumen and an understanding of HR data and analytics—what they are *and how to apply them*.

LEVELING UP WITH DATA AND ANALYTICS

I remember the first time I learned about HR data and analytics. I was working in a position where I had, as per usual, asked for more responsibility. I wanted to take on more work as a means to grow my knowledge and skills (sometimes you've got to be careful what you ask for), and I wasn't really prepared for it, but I was certainly given more responsibility. My new challenge was to help select, then implement, a new Applicant Tracking System (ATS) and I put my all into that project.

I was soaking up more information than I'd ever learned before about our Human Resources Information System (HRIS), our recruiting process, and even how systems "talk" to each other as data is transferred. The ATS would connect with our HRIS, and once we selected a candidate and their offer was accepted, we could click a button to convert them to a new hire. Boom, magic! They'd be in our HRIS, and from there, the new employee would receive a link to complete their new hire paperwork. It's quite standard, of course, but I hadn't seen anything like it prior to that project.

While learning about systems integration was fascinating, something else in this process sparked an awakening for me. During the project, as we reviewed vendors, I noticed my boss at the time would ask questions about each vendor's capabilities regarding measurements. These measurements were things I'd honestly never thought to track.

There I was, sitting at a conference table with my manager and our team, on a conference call with a fantastic vendor who shall not be named. I was taking notes when my manager asked if the system provided data on applicant sources, time-to-fill, and more. As I was writing, my head started spinning.

Oh no, I thought. *I've never once asked the vendors we've been reviewing these questions.* It then occurred to me this data would be extremely helpful in determining if our talent acquisition strategies were effective.

Applicant source data would help us understand where our best (and worst) applicants were coming from. Were they applying mostly via CareerBuilder? Monster? Somewhere else? Then we could use that data to make better decisions about *where* we chose to post our job ads. We could save money on job postings and labor if we cut out ineffective sources.

Time-to-fill data would be extremely beneficial as well. If we had data on how long certain positions took to fill, we could take a deeper look at the reasons for it. We could find out if there was an issue with the recruiting process. We could determine if perhaps a manager over a specific department didn't prioritize interviews and took too long to schedule and complete them, causing us to lose great candidates. Maybe it would give us an indication if we were competitive enough in the market, and we could review our total rewards strategies and how we communicated compensation and benefits in our job ads.

It occurred to me in that moment collecting and analyzing data within HR was just as important as collecting and analyzing data in any other business function. *Duh.* If I could go back and smack my previous self, I would.

After that, I scoured Google, picked the brain of my manager, and did whatever I could to find out more information on HR data and analytics.

I'm disclosing this rather embarrassing story because this is part of the issue. I'm not the only one who was completely unfamiliar with this at some point. Many HR professionals lack skills in data and analytics even today, which contributes to HR's perceived inability to be strategic. Accurate information isn't just useful for making effective decisions; it's critical.

Whenever you're faced with a decision in your personal life, whether large or small, you generally want as much information about it as possible, right? To make an informed decision, data is important. You wouldn't buy a house in a new neighborhood without knowing all the pertinent details. You'd want answers to questions like, is this an area with high crime? What are the property taxes in this area? Are there good schools for the kids?

How many of us check out the reviews for a product prior to purchasing it? We want to know, before forking over our hard-earned cash, we aren't going to regret it. Is the product good quality and effective? Will it do everything it claims to? What's the return policy if something doesn't quite meet expectations?

Having data helps us make informed decisions and be *intentional* in our strategies. Sure, we can take a fly by the seat of our pants approach that relies primarily on our knowledge and expertise, and sometimes this works out well. However, though some guesswork may be involved in devising an effective people strategy (no one has a crystal ball to see *exactly* what will happen), having data to help you forecast business needs and challenges gives you an advantage.

Using data to inform your strategies takes your work to the next level.

As Alexander Alonso, PhD, SHRM-SCP, and Chief Knowledge Officer for SHRM, told me, "Sometimes data isn't always numbers, sometimes it's facts, sometimes it's other information." It's important to keep this in mind when we are thinking about data within our HR strategies. Data *can* be feedback from any number of sources and might even come from your past experiences with a similar situation. The bottom line is understanding and applying data and analytics within HR is here, and we need to embrace it.

In an article titled "Why HR Data Is the Key to Strategic Business Decisions," Meghan M. Biro wrote, "In data lies the future of human resources and talent management." She continued on to say though some progress is being made in the use of data and analytics within HR, more organizations than ever are making the connection between workforce performance and business data. She pointed out HR must make "data-driven business decisions and develop a workforce plan that optimizes talent investments while effectively monitoring recruiting, development, engagement, productivity, accountability, [and] retention."

Deloitte's 2017 Human Capital Trends report showed 71 percent of companies saw people analytics as a high priority, but progress had been lagging, as those companies that were "correlating HR data to business outcomes, performing predictive analytics, and deploying enterprise scorecards barely changed" from the previous year. In Meghan Biro's article, she pointed out Deloitte's 2020 Global Human Capital Trends report showed "53 percent of organizations reported that their leaders' interest in workforce information has increased in the past eighteen months."

Erik van Vulpen, Founder of AIHR, wrote in his 2019 article, titled "The Impact of People Analytics and the Growing Skills Gap," that "Everyone who is using people analytics in their work is aware that there is a divide between people who get people analytics and those who lag behind." He cited some great information in his article that helped illustrate the data and analytics skills gap, such as Cornell University's research report titled "State of HR Analytics," which showed "only 27 percent [of respondents] felt they had a strong team of analytics talent who could execute HR analytics projects, [and] frontline HR generalists failed to understand the value of HR analytics. Only 33 percent thought they would."

Vulpen further pointed out a Corporate Research Forum study conducted in 2017 titled "Research Report: Strategic Workforce Analytics" found only 1 percent of respondents strongly agreed with the statement "HR in my organization is good at analyzing a wide range of both HR and business data before making decisions."

Look, I could go on with more research on the data and analytics skills gap and provide you with statistics for days. Instead, I want to share some insight into this and other skill gaps from Alexander Alonso, PhD, SHRM-SCP, (the Chief Knowledge Officer for SHRM I mentioned a few paragraphs ago). If there is anyone to ask about skills gaps in HR professionals, it's this guy. I had the privilege of speaking to him about this very topic.

HR'S KNOWLEDGE GAPS

I asked him if there are any significant knowledge gaps he was seeing among HR professionals that might be holding us, and our profession as a whole, back. He identified three standout gaps:

- Data and analytics
- Inclusion and equity thinking
- Experience building

On data, Alex said, "It's not necessarily the interpretation [of data that is the problem]…it's about asking the right questions. I can find a lot of HR professionals who understand the value of analytics, but it's asking the right question and understanding what data you need to answer that question that trips people up left and right."

Recently, Alex interviewed CEOs and CHROs from sixty-plus organizations and found when CEOs thought of the strategic ability of HR, one of the components was HR's use of data. CEOs want HR to be data-driven, "so they either use data to help them make decisions, meaning they're using people analytics, or they're using data from other places to really drive what it is they're doing."

The other gaps he identified in his research included inclusion and equity thinking that is data-driven and experience building. He said, "HR needs to get a refresher on what it is that they need to actually measure [with] inclusion and equity. [HR should] focus on what it means to actually invest in inclusion and equity, how well [your organization] does this, and what your workforce and customers think of [your efforts]."

In terms of experience building, Alex saw this as another significant skills gap. He likened crafting the employee experience to that of a marketer's job crafting the customer experience. "Marketers build the consumer journey and the journey for [stakeholders]. The stakeholder that's lost is the employee and the employment experience. I would love to see HR professionals actually build some [marketer] skills that [build] employment experience in a way that represents the consumer experience [and] how you want your consumers to be treated."

Data and analytics are commonly known skills gap with HR professionals, and in 2020, we definitely began to see more emphasis on diversity, inclusion, and equity initiatives. When speaking with other HR professionals and business leaders, I've found other commonly cited skills gaps include relationship building, strategic thinking ability, and surprisingly, a general lack of confidence in seeing oneself as a business leader instead of a paper-pusher. We'll explore these concerns throughout this book, beginning with the employee experience (in terms of being employee-centric) in the next chapter.

Overall, any of these gaps can account for an HR practitioner's impediment to being a true strategic partner in business. When we aren't performing as a strategic partner in HR, we are self-perpetuating the idea some hold that HR is merely a tactical, administrative function. It's imperative we rise above this notion by showing our ability to be strategic and intentional.

Of course, one of the biggest skills gaps outside of those mentioned above is a lack of business acumen. Business acumen encompasses a broad knowledge of business. It requires an individual to "get" how business works. Ask yourself these questions:

- Do you understand the ins and outs of what makes up your organization's financial performance?
- Are you familiar with consumer trends that relate to your industry?

- Who is your client/customer base?
- What political and environmental factors affect your organization?
- Who are your competitors?
- What are your growth strategies?

These are examples of questions someone with at least some business acumen should be able to answer.

I can't even remember the last time I opened an actual encyclopedia (we do have the Internet now, after all), so I'll share with you the definition of "business acumen" and what it means to have business acumen skills per Indeed.com's editorial team: "Business acumen, sometimes referred to as business sense or business savvy, is a person's ability to understand various business scenarios and cope with them effectively. People with strong business acumen skills can better understand business issues, adapt and remain flexible during times of change, comprehend business operations, and provide quality insight as to how to achieve goals and ensure business success."

As Brian Summerfield pointed out in a 2008 *Chief Learning Officer Magazine* article titled "A Crisis in Leadership," business acumen has also "emerged as a vehicle for improving financial performance and leadership." To really boil it down, business acumen is all about seeing the big picture. As Kevin Cope, Founder of Acumen Learning, puts it in his book *Seeing the Big Picture*, business acumen is about knowing "how the key drivers of the business relate to each other, work together to produce profitable growth, and relate to the job."

You can have all the people data you could ever wish for at your fingertips. Without an understanding of the business and how the people function affects it, that data becomes useless, as you won't be able to effectively analyze and use that data for decision-making. We must have business acumen and we must use that to be *intentional* with strategies that drive the business.

THE ELUSIVE SEAT AT THE TABLE

Throughout my time as a consultant, I've worked with organizations that have no internal HR representation, as well as those that do. Some have one HR professional while larger clients sometimes have an entire HR department. A common thread I've observed from the HR professionals I've worked with (whether they're a department of one or even a director leading an HR team) is the frustration they feel when they don't have that "seat at the table."

I build relationships with my clients and many have felt comfortable sharing these frustrations with me and asking for guidance. In some instances, the professionals frustrated that they aren't perceived as strategic are getting in their own way. They don't always realize it, but they are perpetuating this notion themselves.

I remember one client I had in a previous role as a consultant. He was an HR director at a professional services firm, and he shared with me though there was no one above him in HR, his inclusion in strategic planning meetings with his executive team was lacking. When he first joined the company, he was initially involved in all strategic meetings, but over the years, this inclusion became increasingly rare. Once, the executives even began making major changes to the company's benefits offering during the front end of their annual renewal discussions without even telling him.

During our talk about his frustration (and contemplation about moving to another company), we discovered in his case, the reason why he had been cut out over time was his own doing and he hadn't recognized it as it was happening. His executive team valued his contributions but didn't see him as strategic. When he came to leadership meetings in his first year with the company, he didn't attempt to propose meaningful people strategies that would help move the needle forward for the business, and he wasn't actively forecasting any potential opportunities or challenges.

He was very knowledgeable in compliance and employee relations but took a very reactive approach instead of a proactive one.

When we show our colleagues we are only focused on the tactical aspects of HR or the administrative facets, we aren't going to be taken seriously as strategic thinkers. When we are reactive to situations instead of anticipating them and proactively coming up with solutions, we aren't being intentional. We lose our value as a strategic player. We have to ensure we are focused on the right things and *act* as strategic partners in order for ourselves and the HR function to be valued and *seen* as strategic.

When HR doesn't drive strategy (and many HR professionals don't), we are part of the problem that causes us so much frustration. We are contributing to an us versus them mentality. We see it all the time with employees; they think we are the fun police, or that we are only there to cover the employer's ass. When we *are* strategic drivers, we create positive business impacts, both for the employees and for the employer. Being strategic in HR helps to break down the us versus them perception across the board—from line employees to the C-suite.

Recently, I spoke with Fabia Bourda, MBA, SPHR, SHRM-SCP, PMP. She is a global human resources consultant with over twenty-five years of experience working with Fortune 500 C-suite executives. We were discussing the perception of HR being tactical versus strategic, and the frustration many HR professionals feel when they encounter this.

She started with telling me, "Oftentimes, companies don't have the opportunity to really think about [HR strategies] and what they're able to do. Part of it is a financial consideration. HR is a cost center, so naturally, [executives may not want] to put out money [for HR initiatives] unless they actually *mean* something." Fabia said this could be due to a company's size in some cases.

Smaller organizations may not have resources to devote to having a strategic HR function. In these instances, she said HR naturally becomes "very tactical and reactive in what [they're] doing. Large organizations have the luxury of having more people, and people dedicated to focus around more strategic topics." In organizations lacking the resources to devote to HR strategies and initiatives, HR professionals are forced to be more reactive instead of looking to the future, even if they are very well trained and great strategic thinkers.

However, it's important to keep trying to push for a more proactive, intentional strategic approach to help your leadership understand the value of the HR function. It might take more work than you'd like to be seen as a strategic partner, but the alternative is settling in and accepting your fate as a tactical paper-pusher. Who wants that?

Fabia shared a story of how she worked for a company and encountered this sort of us versus them mentality from leadership that didn't view HR for what it truly was. "I remembered when I was head of HR [there]. They hated HR. The [leadership team] came from a consulting firm and all the executives hated HR, but they knew it was a 'necessary evil.' They had certain expectations of what I was supposed to do and they really weren't getting it. So, one of the things I would do is put together, every two weeks, all the different types of employee relations issues [we had]." This gave her leadership team a deeper understanding of issue areas.

However, Fabia made sure to also provide the executives with forecasts and information on how those issues were impacting the company's financial performance. That's when her executives started to make the connection that HR makes a big difference to the bottom line. Fabia used business acumen to tie the people issues to the company's bottom line. That was the moment her executive team began to understand HR more as a strategic function.

To be seen as a strategic partner, Fabia suggested ensuring you first understand your industry and the work your organization performs. This way, your strategies will be meaningful to your organization specifically. She also suggested you keep learning and developing your business acumen. Finally, she said we must make it a priority to inform executives of what is currently important within our people operations, as well as what executives need to think about for the future. "In HR, we must understand how to provide valuable information to business leaders. Until you can provide that, you're powerless."

Fabia continued, "It's really about value you can add, alignment with the organization, and what [leaders are] expecting. You can't make them change their mind, but you can provide them with the right level of context and detail that they need and be supportive…that's the way to get in." Executives and business leaders don't see HR as strategic when we lack in business acumen, don't embrace the digital age with data and analytics, and don't drive strategy.

We perpetuate this notion when we don't educate our leaders on the strategic value of HR. We perpetuate this when we don't take the time to improve our skills and be proactive and intentional in our people initiatives.

HR makes a difference, and to get our seat at the table, we have to show it.

PART 2

HR STRATEGY IS MORE CRITICAL TODAY THAN EVER BEFORE

CHAPTER 6

People Centricity

"There's always an opportunity with crisis. Just as it forces an individual to look inside himself, it forces a company to reexamine its policies and practices."

—JUDY SMITH

Are you tired of virtual meetings yet? Are you lying awake at night worried about retaining your top talent? Does your mind race as you continue coming up with fresh and innovative ways to motivate and engage your workforce? Are you absolutely exhausted trying to keep up with regulatory changes; burned out from policy revisions and shifting your workforce between virtual and office formats?

You aren't alone.

It's become clear since the beginning of the global COVID-19 pandemic that effective people strategies, driven by strategic HR professionals, are more important now than ever before. The way in which we have seemingly always worked has been redefined due to COVID-19. On top of that, we've seen changing expectations among different generations in the workforce. We know businesses need the right people, in the right positions, doing the right things to thrive and grow, even outside of a global pandemic.

HR is all about the *people* in the business, and therefore holds much of the responsibility for this. We hire, train, develop, and work to retain talent. All of this is done while simultaneously implementing strategies that align the people in an organization to the overall goals of the company. It's a bit of a juggling act to say the least.

While many of us never endeavored to become circus performers, learning to juggle our HR responsibilities is a necessity. Why? HR must align people strategies with organizational strategies to create a competitive advantage for the business. That competitive advantage ideally results in higher revenues. Businesses are about making money; that's the whole point. Sure, there are businesses that are also social ventures aimed at bettering their communities and society, but let's be real—overwhelmingly, businesses exist for the purpose of maximizing owner and shareholder profits through offering, for a price, their products and/or services.

Welcome to capitalism.

CUSTOMER CENTRICITY
Long ago, businesses found to be more profitable, they must become customer focused, or customer-*centric*. You've probably heard that phrase before: customer-centric. It's been a buzzword for quite a while. Maybe you've heard "the

customer is always right" (*not* true, by the way, at least in my opinion and that of the fine folks working retail jobs), but what does it mean?

To be brief, customer-centricity, or being customer-centric, means focusing on your customers to become more profitable—understanding how they think, listening to their feedback, and designing your business around the customers. It's a simple but powerful premise. Without customers to buy your products and services, the business goes bust. To obtain and retain customers, you need to know what they want, how they want it, when they want it, *and* have exceptional customer service.

This wasn't always evident. It was figured out over time through efforts to increase sales via marketing strategies. Andy Hasselwander gives a great history of customer-centricity in an article for MarketBridge. Per his article in the 1960s, there was a marketing revolution. Instead of mass media campaigns (radio and TV ads), marketers began focusing on *individual* users/customers in efficient and relevant ways, like direct mail campaigns. Social science was incorporated into business practices and market research was centered on customer trends.

He continued along the timeline within his article and explained the next change in marketing came awhile later. In the 1980s and 1990s, more tracking of customer behaviors started rolling out. For example, loyalty programs and rewards cards that would track customer buying and provide targeted offers were introduced. Also, in the 1990s, thanks to the Internet and the rise in e-commerce toward the end of the decade, even more opportunities became available for a business to really understand their customers and reach them with targeted ads.

Since then, social media has made it even easier to target tailored ads to customers and gather data on individual buying habits. This is why it feels like the mere second I mention to my husband I'm thinking of buying a new curling iron, I'll see an ad pop up for one in my social media feeds.

For quite some time now, businesses have been *very* customer-centric. I'm not arguing this isn't important—it is—but this customer-centricity should start at home. By home, I mean within the business, with its *internal* customers—specifically its employees.

Some businesses prioritize customers to the detriment of their employees, putting customers or clients first before employee satisfaction, wellbeing, or even safety. Don't we all know someone who's worked somewhere like this? Many of us have worked in this sort of place ourselves. If we haven't, we certainly see horror stories in the news about it. Places like a certain former bookstore turned global juggernaut online retailer, for example.

If you have worked somewhere like this, I feel your pain. I've been there, and it's *so* not a good time.

It's easy to understand how this can happen. Remember, the whole point of business is to make money. When leaders become focused on increasing profits, sometimes that focus comes with blinders to other matters like the wellbeing of employees. In times of financial stress, a business (especially a small one) can easily fall into this kind of hyper focus. That tunnel vision often leads to decisions that impact employees in a negative way. In many cases, it may easily include things like reductions in force and leaner operations, higher workloads, reduced benefits and pay, and rewarding behavior that results in financial gain alone, even if that behavior is bad.

Eva Rykrsmith shared this experience in a blog post for QuickBase.com. She said one of her first jobs had this extreme customer-centric approach where management made customers top priority at the expense of the employees. While Rykrsmith didn't elaborate with an example, I took the liberty of imagining some of the issues faced by employees. In my mind, I envisioned employees working with no breaks to meet unrealistic sales or services goals. I also pictured employees forced to take verbal abuse from customers who are questioning their bill or looking for a refund or exchange, with no support or anyone stepping in from management.

I may have an overactive imagination, but sadly, this is the reality for far too many workers. Rykrsmith details how her employer's laser focused customer-centric approach resulted in a culture that bred unhappy employees who were unable to provide great customer service due to their state of mind at work. That kind of dissatisfaction on the job leads to poor performance, disengagement, low morale, and eventually, as was the case for Rykrsmith, retention problems, as employees will eventually leave for greener pastures.

Rykrsmith then referenced a video of Colleen Barrett, President Emeritus of Southwest Airlines and the first woman to serve as president of a major airline. In the video, taken at the twelfth annual Wharton Leadership Conference, Barrett shared that Southwest did things a bit differently. She said, "At the top of our pyramid, in terms of priority, is our employees and delivering to them proactive customer service. If we do a good enough job of that, they in turn spend their time trying to assure the second most important group on our pyramid—our passengers—feel good about the services they are getting. And if those people feel good enough about it, then they come back for more."

When a business focuses on their customers, understands what they want, and increases customer satisfaction, they naturally increase profits. Southwest gets it. Barrett's words and Rykrsmith's story are excellent illustrations of why customer-centricity should begin with employee-centricity. If you want your employees to provide excellent service and focus on your customers, then you need to provide those employees with excellent service internally. Take good care of them while building a positive culture that keeps employees happy, loyal, and engaged.

EMPLOYEE CENTRICITY

So, what exactly is employee-centricity? A writer named Ashish defined it in simple terms in a blog post he wrote for Culturo.com. "Each employee is valued and viewed as important to the company's success in achieving its shared vision and mission." So basically, an *employee-centric* organization takes the concept of *customer-centricity* and applies it to employees. Focusing on the employees in a way that ensures happy staff and in turn, happy customers.

In another article on the topic, a Business.com member defined employee-centricity in terms of company culture, writing that employee-centricity was "an environment where ideas, creativity, free-flowing communication, and innovation are encouraged throughout an organization. Employees...feel safe to make suggestions and challenge the inner workings they may feel are interfering with productivity and performance." The author went on to explain employee-centric cultures fostered employees who felt a sense of pride in the business.

When an employee feels that kind of connection to their job, a sense of belonging, purpose, and pride in the company, they want to see the company succeed. That's when they will go the extra mile in their role to make it happen.

Research shows customer satisfaction is built more effectively through focusing on employees first. In a fascinating Inc.com article, David Burkus shared that over twenty years ago, Harvard University business professors W. Earl Sasser, Leonard Schlesinger, James Heskett, Thomas Jones, and Gary Loveman worked to combine and synthesize their own research with that of others on this topic. They were able to build a model that explained the success of the most profitable service-based businesses. Originally published in 1994, their work was detailed in a *Harvard Business Review* article, "Putting the Service-Profit Chain to Work," and here's what happened.

W. Earl Sasser had researched with a former student, Fred Reichheld, the common assumption held at the time (we're talking about the mid-1990s here) that the primary factor of profitability was market share. However, they found this was just one factor, and customer loyalty was another. Using their research, they were able to estimate a 5 percent increase in customer loyalty could yield a staggering 25 to 85 percent increase in profitability.

Using this research as a starting point, the group of Harvard professors began a search to find out what drives customer loyalty. They combed through available research, studied dozens of successful businesses, and created a model to identify those customer loyalty drivers. Named the "service-profit chain," the model included several "links" from internal service quality, employee satisfaction, all the way to customer loyalty and revenue growth/profitability.

The service-profit chain includes elements of a business model that show a linear connection, and here it is:

A high perception of service value drives customer satisfaction. That perception of value is derived from productive employees. Employees are productive when they are happy (satisfied).

While what determines an employee's happiness and satisfaction may vary among individuals, generally speaking, happy or satisfied employees are ones who get their needs met through rewarding work, fair pay, benefits, and feeling respected and valued. This is in addition to feeling a sense of purpose, connection, and belonging within the organization. For some employees, it may also include professional development and/or promotion opportunities.

To break it down, as Burkas wrote in his article, customer loyalty drives profits. Customer loyalty is caused by employee satisfaction. Employee satisfaction results from putting employees first. So, if putting employees first *before* customers results in higher customer satisfaction and loyalty, which in turn results in some huge increases in profitability, how exactly does an organization put employees first?

Jack Altman is the CEO and Cofounder of Lattice, a people management platform focused on employee engagement and culture. Altman helps to define and outline this in his book, *People Strategy: How to Invest in People and Make Culture Your Competitive Advantage*. As he explains it, a people-centric organization is one where the company "believes that people are at the center of everything they do,"—specifically employees. He calls employees the "foundation upon which all other business strategies are predicated," and I completely agree.

Putting employees at the center of everything your organization *does* means focusing on culture, development, and employee engagement. This doesn't mean you have to bend to every desire of your employees, and it doesn't mean everyone gets a massive corner office just to keep them happy. Putting employees first means prioritizing culture, engagement, and their development instead of letting these endeavors fall to the wayside as you become laser focused on the profit and loss statement. This makes people strategies, and therefore HR, just as important to a company's bottom line as sales and marketing, if not more so.

Prioritizing putting employees first drives profitability and customer satisfaction and provides other benefits to employers as well. When your organization is truly employee-centric, employees are likely to enjoy working there. This results in a reduction in costly turnover and retaining valuable company knowledge. For those who may not know the real cost of turnover, just take a look at the data compiled in Shane McFeely and Ben Wigert's article for the renowned research organization, Gallup.

They wrote, "The cost of replacing an individual employee can range from one-half to two times the employee's annual salary," and they considered that estimate to be on the conservative side. They went on to say, "A one-hundred-person organization that provides an average salary of 50 thousand dollars could have turnover and replacement costs of approximately 660 thousand to 2.6 million dollars per year." That's costly indeed.

In addition to avoiding turnover, when an employee is happy, they are much more likely to refer others to your business as a great place to work.

Have you ever been unhappy at a job and felt like the company's leaders really didn't care about the staff at all? When working for that company, did you refer anyone to open positions, or did you warn them not to apply instead? Personally, I would never tell a friend or talented colleague to join a company if I felt the leaders treated their employees like crap or didn't care to put them first.

When employees are taken care of, it elevates your employer brand and helps you attract top talent. I remember, many years ago, I found myself on the hunt for a new job. I was already employed, but I wanted more growth opportunities and I very much wanted to land a job at a large local eyecare company. I wasn't exactly passionate about the eyecare products they manufactured, but their reputation as a great place to work was well-known. Anyone I spoke with in the area spoke highly of the company.

Employees were paid well and were provided with clear career development paths. In addition, work/life balance was prioritized, and teams were encouraged to be creative and innovative. The competition to get a job at this company was, and still is, fierce. I ended up moving and never applied, but I do remember watching their job postings almost religiously for quite some time, hoping to see something in HR pop up.

This recipe for success is powerful but sadly underutilized. Building an excellent company culture where employees are put first leads to higher engagement, which leads to higher productivity and profitability.

Why wouldn't you put employees first?

To be clear, there are some folks out there who feel "putting employees first" is either too expensive or would result in disaster, as employees are given free rein to "run the ship." I remember an old client of mine, when I was an HR consultant in a prior role, who had this notion.

When I became their HR consultant, this client wasn't all that interested in what I could do for them. They had signed up for my company's services for the payroll processing and benefits. HR consulting was just part of the package and they didn't expect to use it. This was a company of about two hundred employees. This client went through the motions and allowed me to inquire about their current HR practices and what issues they were experiencing. Overall, I could tell they weren't interested in anything I could do for them—at first.

Through my inquires, I found they were having major issues with talent acquisition and retention. Most employees were leaving in under a year, typically under six months. When I crunched the numbers for them and revealed how much these issues were costing the company, it was a wakeup call. That's when their tune changed. "Can you find out what we are doing wrong here? Why doesn't anyone want to come work for us? Why do so many employees leave so quickly?"

I got to work.

I did all the usual things. I surveyed employees on their satisfaction, reviewed their talent acquisition strategies and total rewards package, etc. The catalyst for the company's issues was glaringly obvious to me. It came up time and again in the employee's survey responses and in the feedback I received when interviewing members of middle management. Simply put, the employees didn't come first. They didn't even come second. They were dead last. The benefits they had were decent, but the pay wasn't great. "They should expect that in this industry," my client said. The pay might have been on par with market compensation data, but leaders were sending a message to the staff that they weren't valued.

This message was prevalent within the company culture. The work environment was almost oppressing, the staff felt the employer was punitive over even the tiniest of things, and the leadership team had some ridiculous standards and a general lack of empathy for the staff as humans.

To illustrate, a woman had been terminated for missing *one* shift. She had no history of being a no call, no show and she didn't have a previous attendance problem. In her history with the company, she had only been tardy one time when she had some car trouble. The reason she was a no call, no show? Her father had passed away that day at the breakfast table, with her and the rest of their immediate family present. It was sudden and so, of course, she missed work. Her mind wasn't on calling in for her shift, it was on calling an ambulance to try and save her father's life. She followed the ambulance to the hospital where she received the worst news of her life.

This was just one example. It's a bit of a severe one, but sadly, it happened, and this treatment was on par with how the employees were treated all the time. Needless to say, no one wanted to work there because they'd earned a reputation as a terrible employer.

Raising employee wages and leading the market in comp and benefits wasn't going to make a dent in their issue. They needed to change their treatment of employees and their company culture. Nearly everything leadership implemented communicated to the employees they were not valued. I showed my findings to the leadership team, along with an overview of how these issues were causing them to suffer financially. I also shared research on how employee-centricity benefits the bottom line.

Finally, they were on board to make a change. Ideally, employers would want to take an employee-centric approach just because it's the right thing to do. For this client, it took more; they needed to see and understand the financial impact. Over time, with the strategies I developed and helped to implement to change their culture, the company saw significant improvement. Some members of leadership were still initially resistant to the new direction of management practices and company policies. Those who were hesitant to embrace the changes assumed employees would be running amok and doing whatever they wanted.

Much to their surprise (not mine), that's not what happened. Employees were being heard and they started to feel valued. Then, the staff became more willing to listen to management than ever before and employees no longer felt management was their enemy. In the end, they embraced moving to an employee-centric culture and they were very happy for my HR consulting services. Employee retention improved, as did their ability to attract new talent, and their revenues increased along with improvements in their customer service.

The moral of the story? Some may think being employee-centric is too costly. Some might think it means employees can do whatever they want without consequences, tying the hands of the employer, but it's just a myth. Driving HR strategies that affect the wellbeing of employees in a positive way is a wise move. This is a great way to be *intentional* in your HR role.

Be the hero who improves employee engagement and, in turn, productivity and customer service. After all, employee-centricity is undoubtedly vital for your employer brand and your bottom line.

CHAPTER 7

The Human in Human Resources

"Treat a person as he is, and he will remain as he is. Treat a person as if he were where he could be and should be, and he will become what he could be and should be."

—JIMMY JOHNSON

You know what's a terrible name? Human resources. Yep, I said it.

Think about it, though. *Human resources.* For one thing, there's no pizazz to it. Sure, we in HR deal with *humans,* and we provide them with *resources,* but that's not the way many business professionals think of human resources. Really, it means we are working with the company's most expensive and important resources or assets: the humans the organization employs.

The name almost makes it sound like employees are synonymous to raw goods, or the machines we use to manufacture products, or the technology we use in our work. Humans are just another resource. Calling our profession and our department *human resources* doesn't exactly bring the warm fuzzies, does it? After all, we know humans aren't just a resource. People aren't robots.

We've talked about how employee-centricity makes a positive impact to the bottom line. However, treating people as people (and not like robots) is more than just beneficial for financial reasons. It's the right thing to do. I mean, who wants to be that jerk who views staff members as just another number? Does anyone like that guy? No!

Additionally, people *expect* to be treated as humans. Times have changed. What employees want from their employer has changed, and we'll explore more of that in the next chapter. For now, let's dive more into how HR is responsible for people strategies that impact an organization's ability to reach their goals and achieve their mission and vision.

HR is all about the people and must be strategic and *intentional* when it comes to culture, engagement, productivity, and more.

TREATING PEOPLE AS PEOPLE DRIVES ENGAGEMENT
Have you ever felt like you were just a number at work, or perhaps your manager didn't care about you? Maybe you knew no matter how good of a job you did, it was just never enough.

Have you felt if something happened to you, it wouldn't be any skin off your boss's back to replace you? I've felt that way.

I won't say where I was working at the time, but I once had a boss like that a long time ago. This boss was condescending whenever she spoke to any employee, though she didn't acknowledge us unless she had to. That's right, no "hello," "good morning," "how are you," nada. In fact, she would reprimand employees if they so much as spoke to each other about anything that wasn't 100 percent work-related. This wasn't in response to an office gossip problem either. This was the way she managed her team.

Team building activities that would foster employee relationships and collaboration? Forget about it; unheard of. Five minutes late to work because you had a flat tire? Not her problem, and you better believe she would ding you for it in your performance evaluation, even if it was a one-time occurrence and you'd never been late to work or missed a shift the rest of the year.

I was miserable going into work at that job. Some days, I would look at my babies as I dropped them off at daycare and think to myself, *I'm doing this for you. I'm putting myself through this hell for you.* My kids were the only reason I kept going into work. The pay and benefits were decent, and I wanted to be able to provide the best for my children. Over time, despite my glowing performance reviews and raises, the situation never improved. It only got worse.

The day after my outstanding evaluation, where I had been rated as exceeding expectations in every category, I was berated. Why, you ask? I hadn't yet made an entry into our HRIS regarding an executive employee's leave of absence request. The reason I hadn't? It turned out the executive wouldn't be taking a leave after all. I showed my e-mail correspondence with the executive and explained the situation to my manager. "Oh," she said. "Okay then." That was it. No apology for yelling at me and screaming about her team's incompetence. Not a word about how she didn't need to micromanage me, as evidenced by my amazing performance review. Not to mention the fact I was on top of this and had proactively reached out to the executive to get the leave details squared away.

I cried on my way home that day. I'd reached my limit. The next day, I gave my notice and told myself I wouldn't work that hard for an employer who didn't truly value me. Pay raises and promotions are great, but they no longer meant anything to me if I didn't feel appreciated and wasn't treated with basic respect and decency.

It came from the top. This kind of management permeated throughout leadership and the entire organization. Did we have a problem with turnover? You bet. Declining performance? Uh huh, absolutely. Did all of our issues culminate in the loss of customer orders and contracts? Yep. That, in turn, caused a sequence of layoffs as the company attempted to stabilize their continued losses.

In contrast, I've also experienced amazing management and a company culture that was employee-centric. At that company, employees were treated as people and the organization made an effort to show employees their appreciation. One of their strategies was to recognize employee contributions through spot bonus programs, along with other recognition and rewards opportunities. You could provide suggestions at any time, even anonymously, and management asked for feedback in weekly meetings.

Executives also had monthly townhalls where they would review employee input. In those townhalls, employees were provided with information on the trends management saw in the feedback we gave them. The executives paid special attention to any concerning feedback they received, and they explained how feedback would be used. Best of all, they meant it. It wasn't just the standard lip service so many organizations take part in. We were able to see many of our suggestions implemented, and our input was taken seriously. Leadership communicated with employees in a transparent way that was refreshing.

While working at this job, I became very ill. Not just *I've got the flu and I'll be out for a week* ill, but *I'm spending weeks in the hospital and it's scary* ill. Once I was admitted to the hospital, managers contacted me to check on me first and foremost. Then I was told I needn't worry, they were putting me on a paid leave of absence (I wasn't yet eligible for FMLA) and they'd work with me as much as possible. Assuming I wouldn't be out for six months or more, my job was still mine as soon as I was healthy enough to work.

I appreciated their care and how they handled my illness. Once I was healthy again and back to work, I made it a mission to work even harder. I was later approached by a recruiter about a job that would've been a promotion with more money and better benefits at another company. At my family's urging, I did check it out and had an interview. I was offered the job but ended up turning it down.

My current company had really taken care of me. I liked my coworkers, our leadership team, and our culture. It would take a lot more than what was offered to get me to leave. The offer I received would've made a significant difference for my family. However, I'd already learned my lesson. I wanted to be happy at work more than anything else. I preferred to be loyal to my employer and grow my career there. I didn't want to take my chances on a different company culture where employees may not be as valued.

Some companies know the value of effective HR strategies that impact employee engagement and retention and, sadly, others don't. This is why HR must work to be strategic drivers. It's not just fluffy, feel-good stuff we're talking about here. We must be a part of the strategic HR revolution and become more intentional in our work. It has an impact on everyone in the workforce. It matters.

Mary Schaefer, Principal of Artemis Path, Inc., is a coach, trainer, and consultant who specializes in talent development, workplace interactions, and change management. She has a master's degree in HR and the PHR certification, and she knows how much our work in HR matters for employers and individuals. At a TedxWilmington conference in 2014, Mary took the stage to talk about HR strategies in employee engagement, and she provided some mind-blowing data.

In her talk, Schaefer referenced a prior Gallup State of the American Workforce Report, but I'm going to provide some more updated information. In the 2017 State of the American Workforce Report, in large font on the first page, Gallup reported only 33 percent of US workers were engaged at work. This was compared to 70 percent of workers who were engaged at work in the world's best organizations. Schaefer said, "Unskilled and unqualified managers at work are impacting their organizations by 450 billion to 550 billion dollars' worth of productivity annually by undermining employee engagement."

That simply can't be ignored!

You've heard people leave work not because of the work itself, but because of their management, right? This is a great example of the severity of the impact managers make on employee engagement. When management practices, as well as company policies and culture, have the effect of working to disengage employees, the lost productivity has a real cost associated.

Clearly, disengagement is not a unique problem, though it does require a strategic HR solution. During her Tedx Talk, Schaefer told the story of how she made a difference during her twenty-year career at DuPont (that well-known chemical company) through an effective people strategy. The strategy was all about treating people *as people* and not robots.

She began, "Many times, when we talk about human resources, we're talking about that function in an organization that handles the people stuff, right? What I'm here to talk to you about today is putting the human back into human resources. I'm here to talk to you about infusing more humanity back into the workplace, for those human beings who happen to be employees." Schaefer liked to use the term "humanly" when discussing employees, how they're treated, and how to engage them. "Humanly" is a term she distinguished from "humanely."

Humane treatment of employees includes giving them access to meet basic needs, such as water fountains and bathroom breaks. Treating employees "humanly" is much different. "To me, for employers to treat employees humanly, it's to address the very human needs [of employees], such as the need to be appreciated, the need to belong, and the need to feel like you're making a meaningful contribution."

According to Schaefer, DuPont didn't have a very humanly view of employees during her time there. She shared that shop floor employees (line workers handling chemicals) were not viewed as people who had any ambition to progress in their careers. They weren't seen as "people with hopes and dreams that wanted to learn and grow." At this point, DuPont had been around for what seemed like forever, and they were already successful. Schaefer discovered one day, through a line worker's simple request, there was perhaps a better way to achieve results than the status quo.

She was working as an SAP software implementation project team leader, and several members of the project team were shop floor employees. These employees had valuable knowledge that was absolutely vital to the success of rolling out the raw materials module Schaefer was working on. One of the shop floor employees on the project team asked Schaefer if she would help him with professional development. He, like many others, sought to earn a promotion and advance his career.

"I was more than glad to help him. He didn't report directly to me and I got his supervisor's permission. At the same time, I made the same offer to anyone else on my team who was interested in developing and growing to advance, and three more people took me up on that." As she worked with the shop floor employees, there was no secret special method to it. "I didn't really do anything fancy that you couldn't find in any management book. I think what I might have done a little differently was I believed in these people, and when human beings are treated in a way that they are capable of more, they rise to the occasion."

By simply *believing* in these employees and taking the time to work with them, teach them management skills, and coach them in their careers, Schaefer made an impact. They had previously been viewed only as shop floor employees without any ambition or special skills, but Schaefer was successfully able to help those individuals achieve their goals.

Three of the four employees she worked with were eventually promoted into exempt positions at the plant. One became a supervisor, one went on to travel the world as an SAP consultant, and one became an SAP resource within his division. The latter had started at the plant sweeping the floors.

By challenging the status quo and truly treating employees "humanly," as she called it, Schaefer was able to make a big difference in these workers' lives. This also created more effective human assets to the company. Schaefer's approach with the shop floor workers was very simple, and it worked in her case. I'd argue "humanly" treatment as the heart of your people strategies aimed to address and improve engagement is vital to the success of said strategies.

As Schaefer shared with us, "Researchers have shown when human needs are met for employees at work…the higher the engagement, meaning that people want to be there. And they are…willing to go the extra mile, even when nobody is looking. Higher engagement has been positively correlated to increased profitability."

Schaefer's story shows us if we truly value and believe in people, and we include this in our HR strategies, our workforce and organizations can realize increased engagement, retention, and talent development.

COMBINING PEOPLE STRATEGY WITH CORPORATE SOCIAL RESPONSIBILITY

Taking this a step further, let's talk about HR strategies that combine treating people "humanly" and corporate social responsibility. This is a hot topic in today's world, as more and more people want to know what a company values and what they're really all about. You've seen it in the news: consumers boycotting companies due to their sexual harassment scandals, negative environmental impacts, unfair labor and employment practices, low wages, and more.

Denise Lee Yohn provided us with a great summary on this in an article for the *Harvard Business Review*. She wrote about how IBM was accused of laying off older workers to focus on a younger and "presumably tech savvy" workforce in a class action suit from former employees. She also wrote about Nebraska Furniture Mart. They faced a lawsuit brought by the ACLU for employment ads that specifically targeted young men in blue-collar positions women are generally excluded from. These companies undoubtedly faced backlash from consumers and took a hit to their reputations as employers.

Lee Yohn wrote, "Companies are coming under increased scrutiny from media, customers, investors, and other stakeholders for organizational practices that used to be hidden from the public. Plus, social media gives consumers a voice with which to speak out against companies they believe are unfair or irresponsible—and they expect those companies to listen and respond." This age of cancel culture and social media blasting makes HR strategies and corporate social responsibility more crucial than ever before.

The United Nations Industrial Development Organization (UNIDO) defined Corporate Social Responsibility (CSR) as "a management concept whereby companies integrate social and environmental concerns in their business operations and interactions with their stakeholders. CSR is generally understood as being the way through which a company achieves a balance of economic, environmental, and social imperatives while at the same time addressing the expectations of shareholders and stakeholders."

Corporate social responsibility is widely understood to be strategies that contribute to the employer's reputation and brand. In the journal *Academy of Management*, Abagail McWilliams and Donald Siegel wrote, "CSR goes beyond compliance with regulatory requirements and engages in actions that appear to further some social good, beyond the interests of the firm and that which is required by law."

So how can an HR professional be strategic and keep social responsibility in mind? One way is in addressing the talent shortage (more on the talent shortage in the next chapter). Joe DeLoss, founder of Hot Chicken Takeover, found a way to combine effective HR strategies with corporate social responsibility. At a TEDx Talk in Columbus, Ohio, DeLoss told the story of how, through excellent HR strategy, he was able to make that social impact in his community while building a talent pipeline.

DeLoss considered himself a hustler and entrepreneur since the age of four, but he found himself pulled to volunteering throughout his youth. Through church, social groups, clubs, and other organizations, he picked up trash, organized canned food drives, worked in soup kitchens, and more. In his second year of college, DeLoss was lost and unsure of the direction he wanted to go in. He knew a traditional job wasn't for him, and he wouldn't be successful in such an environment. He also wanted to help others in his community.

DeLoss recognized his position of privilege, knowing not everyone could go to college or even take time to figure out what they really wanted to do. He continued to volunteer but found himself becoming discouraged about taking a path of service in life.

While serving soup in a soup kitchen day after day, he realized nothing was being done to address the heart of the problem. "I [was] getting really discouraged and really depressed...I realized day by day, bowl by bowl, I could keep serving soup, but I'm doing nothing to shorten the line." DeLoss became determined to find a solution to the problems causing the line at the soup kitchen to begin with.

That was where his true calling and path in life finally became clear to him. Through social entrepreneurship, he could combine his love for business and social impact and find long-term, strategic ways to solve problems sustainably.

In 2013, DeLoss and his wife took a babymoon to Nashville, where hot chicken was all the rage. An idea formed, and in April of 2014, Hot Chicken Takeover was born in Columbus, Ohio. Hot Chicken Takeover is a family-style, fried chicken restaurant where patrons can gather together at a table and enjoy an atmosphere not unlike a church potluck or family reunion.

Hot Chicken takeover deliberately hires those who have been affected by the cycle of poverty and experienced homelessness or incarceration. These individuals make up around 65 percent of their employees. DeLoss describes the business impact of tapping into this talent pool, saying, "What we've achieved as an outcome is we have the most reliable, motivated workforce in this community."

He shared a secret with the audience: he didn't really love fried chicken. "What I do love is a little more unusual. I absolutely love human resources. Not many people love HR. I think we've been programmed to resent HR in many ways. But…when I talk about HR, I'm not talking about pink slips, or paperwork, or trust falls." Hot Chicken Takeover has a 50 percent retention rate, which DeLoss claims is four times better than other companies in his industry. This also means this strategy has positively affected HCT's bottom line, as they have spent four times *less* than competitors on rehiring and training employees.

DeLoss wasn't worried about utilizing an underserved candidate pool. While others may shy away from people in poverty or individuals with criminal records, DeLoss embraced them. He pointed out those living in the cycle of poverty were problem solvers, troubleshooters, and capable. These are skills that become key professional assets. "If an employer can build the right culture and infrastructure to harness this power of people, really big things can happen."

To illustrate this further, DeLoss shared a story of an HCT employee. Shannon had been convicted on charges related to theft and drugs and was subsequently incarcerated for five years. However, she made it a point to use her time while incarcerated to improve her future. She found mentors and resources, got sober, and made a plan to put into action upon her release. "We were really grateful we were part of her plan and able to be an employer that was open to bringing her in. Because the way we do it at Hot Chicken is to choose to judge somebody by their future, not by their past, and the outcomes of that are unbelievable."

DeLoss continued, sharing that within six months of beginning her employment with Hot Chicken Takeover, Shannon made great strides in her personal life. She obtained housing and a vehicle and reunited with her son. Professionally, she was promoted five times. HCT even created an administrative role for her where she was responsible for managing the front of the house and handling large amounts of cash. DeLoss said this was a great example of someone who was empowered through their work to take charge of their life, "and we get to benefit from that as an employer."

Through effective talent acquisition, development, and engagement strategies, John positioned Hot Chicken Takeover for success both now and in the future. He tapped an underused talent pool and is reaping the rewards of loyal, high-performing employees while making positive change in his community.

As John said, "I love HR. I believe HR is the single most efficient tool we have to tackle the cycle of poverty, and it's not just about social impact. I believe we have an opportunity to solve an enormous economic problem in our community." I agree, and as HR professionals, we all must rise to the occasion and be strategic partners who impact our organizations and support our corporate social responsibility initiatives.

Part of that social responsibility should start within the organization, specifically with how employees are treated. The way an organization treats its internal and external customers, the impact the organization has within a community (be it positive or negative), and the impact the organization has on the environment, among other things, all work to build the employer's brand and reputation.

Treating people—*all people*—as human beings and not just another number or "resource" can take an organization to new heights. Loyal and engaged workers who feel a sense of purpose and belonging can drive profits through stellar performance, improved customer service, and more.

Earning a reputation as a fair, honest, and socially responsible employer who values and embraces diversity, equity, inclusion, and sustainable practices isn't unrealistic. It just takes some intentional HR strategies.

CHAPTER 8

What Workers Want

"There are no secrets to success. It is the result of preparation, hard work, and learning from failure."

—COLIN POWELL

Having an employee-centric organization and solid people strategies matters now more than ever before, as we've been in a crisis for nearly two years now.

Johnny C. Taylor, Jr. wrote in his new book, *Reset: A Leader's Guide to Work in an Age of Upheaval,* "The upheaval of a crisis forces us all to challenge everything we have been thinking and saying about work on virtually every front. Even organizations that think they have it right discover they need to revisit how they do things. And that's the silver lining of a crisis."

Oh, and what an upheaval we've had. It's been mentioned previously in this book, but let's go ahead and address the elephant in the room—COVID-19—head on. The global pandemic led to massive shifts in the way work is performed and many companies were forced to shift operations to allow remote working from home almost overnight. The pandemic quickly turned business leaders' attention to sustaining operations while keeping workers safe and productive.

In June of 2020, PriceSmart CEO Sherry Bahrambeygui spoke with Wharton management professor Michael Useem about how putting employees first was essential in her company's pandemic response in a virtual event series hosted by Knowledge at Wharton. Per the Association of American Chambers of Commerce in Latin America and the Caribbean (AACCLA), PriceSmart is the largest operator of membership warehouse clubs in Central America and the Caribbean. Bahrambeygui shared how her company quickly pivoted to a remote work environment (for employees whose work allowed it) to protect employees and maintain operations.

They made this enormous shift in work even though PriceSmart had never included remote work in their culture or operations prior to the pandemic. Bahrambeygui said, "The first thing I recognized was that given how highly contagious [COVID-19] was, the ability to protect our employees, and offsite them, and allow for remote work was very important." Prior to the pandemic, the company culture included a mentality that valued showing up at work physically, and the company was very successful. I can imagine transitioning to a remote work environment would be inconceivable had it not been for the pandemic and Bahrambeygui's concern about their employees.

Though Bahrambeygui didn't come to PriceSmart with a background in retail, she credited the focus on putting employees first as essential to the company's success during the pandemic. "Our first priority was our people, and our people meant our employees, their safety, and wellbeing... [after that came] making sure we had the appropriate supply, the flow of goods to get to our members, and mitigating any supply chain disruption." Bahrambeygui believed, "When you take care of [employees], they will take care of your members or your customers. When you take care of those two, your shareholders will be taken care of." This is an excellent example of employee-centricity.

Putting employees and their wellbeing first through implementing safety precautions and employee education put the organization in a position to think outside the box when they turned their attention to operations. After ensuring employee safety, they needed to figure out a way to continue selling their goods with a remote workforce. PriceSmart had been working on implementing online sales for years but hadn't yet finalized this model and pulled the trigger. Shifting employees to offsite work resulted in a need to go live with the online model and finally make it happen. Bahrambeygui said, "In a matter of weeks, we went live on that. Finally, [we were] making sure capital and cash flow and cash management were being closely monitored."

Once employees were moved to remote work, PriceSmart's leadership team met with each other daily to navigate the crisis and Bahrambeygui made sure their HR leader was there every day—as HR should be. That's the seat at the table we're always after. As one of the CEOs who truly understands HR's strategic and vital role, Bahrambeygui knew it was essential to include HR leadership as the company determined what would be best and most effective for employees in terms of safety, communication, and processes.

HR LEADS THE WAY IN TIMES OF CRISIS
When organizations shifted to remote work, HR leaders were naturally thrust into the spotlight. Leaders who may not have genuinely valued HR's strategic role previously found themselves turning to their internal HR teams as well as external consultants for guidance. It was critical to ensure employees were able to work and had all of the equipment and tools they needed to complete their job tasks. It was also essential to ensure workers remained engaged while facing a global pandemic that, frankly, terrified most people.

The terror of the pandemic, the massive shifts in work, and in many cases, the lack of work have taken a mental toll on people everywhere. At its onset, many become fearful. They are fearful of themselves or a loved one contracting the virus, but also about how they would be able to care for children who were now completing school remotely at home. On top of all that, there was plenty of worry regarding work. Would your company survive the pandemic? Would you be laid off?

Suddenly, an extreme amount of stress was placed on people everywhere as we navigated our new world. We wondered if it was safe to leave the house to do something as simple as grocery shopping. We quarantined at home in close quarters. We ached to see family and friends. Many were furloughed or laid off and wondered how they would make ends meet and feed their families. Lives were lost, leaving behind loved ones racked with grief. We were left wondering when this nightmare would end. Even as I wrote this, the pandemic continued.

Though some stress may have subsided as we've become accustomed to our new way of life, we are still in one of the most stressful ages of our time.

When we are stressed, it becomes much harder to be engaged and focused on our work. Stress *can* be a great motivator in low doses, as it pushes us to meet deadlines and can actually improve our performance. However, when we experience a high amount of stress, our performance can take a hit. It also may lead to high levels of anxiety and even depression. The pandemic and subsequent shifts to the way we work and live turned up the stress level to unhealthy levels for a lot of individuals, me included.

HR leaders had their work cut out for them. We were tasked with keeping employees safe and employers compliant with new measures such as the Families First Coronavirus Response Act (FFCRA). HR professionals held the responsibility of figuring out effective means of communication with and for employees. On top of that, we needed to implement methods to retain high levels of employee engagement and a sense of teamwork and community among workers. This was no easy feat when work processes had to change drastically. Now everything that could be done online and shared remotely *was*. Talk about embracing the digital age.

Moving forward, as more people began receiving COVID-19 vaccines, businesses started to bring workers back to the office. When the Delta variant came into our midst, some employers were still postponing the return to onsite work. Even once the pandemic has ended and it's safe to return to work in person, we are going to see more organizations retain a remote workforce. Many companies both large and small have determined employees can be just as productive at home and have decided to capitalize on the cost savings they can have from no longer keeping an office space.

Months into the pandemic, even one of my former employers made the decision to keep employees working from home permanently for this very reason. Everyone was still able to complete their work, and they no longer needed the massive expense of office space all over the country for their fifteen-thousand-plus employees spread over a hundred-plus locations. My own much smaller team of under ten employees worked remotely and loved it. I decided to continue our remote operations for the foreseeable future and didn't renew our office lease.

There will also be hybrid models moving forward, where people come into work a few days a week and work from home other days. For some businesses, some workers may come back to work in the office permanently (depending on their position) while other positions stay remote forever.

Kathryn Vasel, a senior writer at CNN Business, penned an article on the pandemic's lasting impact on work. Vasel wrote "[some businesses] are going all in on remote work" and "Twitter said some employees who want to work from home forever, can." She pointed out that DropBox was even implementing a "virtual first" model, where employees would primarily work from home. Vasel said experts have predicted this virtual work flexibility isn't going away, as "workers have proven they can be productive at home."

Implementing a permanent work from home option may prove to be a key retention strategy for some employers, as we've begun to experience higher than normal turnover in the workforce. Anders Melin and Misyrlena Egkolfopoulou wrote about this in a June 2021 article for Bloomberg Wealth, saying, "As office returns accelerate, some employees may want different options. A May survey of a thousand US adults showed that 39 percent would consider quitting if their employers weren't flexible about remote work. The generational difference is clear: among Millennials and Gen Z, that figure was 49 percent, according to the poll by Morning Consult on behalf of Bloomberg News."

This rise in turnover was forecast earlier in 2021 by several retention and turnover experts. In February of 2021, Achievers Workforce Institute surveyed two thousand employed respondents for their 2021 Engagement and Retention Report. Findings included "a whopping 52 percent of respondents say they will job hunt in 2021—up from 35 percent in 2020." Why such high anticipated turnover? According to the report, "the main reasons for job seeking are better compensation and benefits (35 percent) and better work/life balance (25 percent)."

Natalie Baumgartner, PhD, and Chief Workforce Scientist at Achievers Workforce Institute, said in the report, "HR leaders are facing unique challenges right now and need to prioritize the top factors to improve engagement, retention, and employee satisfaction." Retaining a 100 percent virtual, hybrid, or in-person workforce will require HR professionals to stay committed to people strategies focused on culture, employee engagement, performance management, and development. HR professionals must do this while keeping employees feeling connected.

THE EVOLVING EXPECTATIONS OF EMPLOYEES
Looking beyond the pandemic, what employees want from their employers in general has changed significantly over time. To be competitive and retain talent, employers must adjust, and though the pandemic has no doubt had an effect on what employees of every generation want, namely they are looking for work/life balance and work flexibility.

Although what each individual wants and expects from their employers can vary greatly due to circumstances, values, and motivations unique to each of us, we can still see shifting trends over time. Think about the generations in the workforce. We've got the baby boomers, born between 1946 and 1964, many of whom are still working and haven't yet retired. Next, we have Generation X, born between 1965 and 1980. Then the millennials, of course, who were born between 1981 and 1996, and finally, Generation Z, born between 1997 and 2012.

Each generation has different approaches to work, concerns, and needs they expect to be met by their employer. Designing total rewards packages that appeal to multiple generations and implementing management practices that work for everyone can be a challenge.

We'll start with the baby boomers. The Indeed Editorial Team identified workplace expectations and values of this generation in an article about baby boomers in the workforce titled "Characteristics of 'Baby Boomer' Professionals." They wrote that this generation valued professionalism, competition, visibility, authority earned through experience, and a strong, self-sufficient work ethic. "The baby boomer generation is less likely to embrace remote work or work from home options than younger people. For baby boomers, visibility is everything. This generation wants their manager to see them showing up to work on time every day and working hard until the day ends."

When you consider baby boomers didn't grow up in the digital age with home computers and social media like younger generations in the workforce did, this makes sense. Virtual environments may be more challenging for this generation. To be clear, I'm not saying they aren't capable of adapting, as many are and have. What I'm saying is "face time" (not the iPhone videocalls, but in-person exchanges) is more important for the engagement and morale of this generation. The Indeed article hit the nail on the head when they said, "a workplace geared toward younger people can isolate older generations." This is especially true when working in a completely virtual format.

What do baby boomers want from employers? For one thing, they want stability and longevity. This generation didn't hop from job to job. Indeed shared baby boomers "take pride in the companies they work for, the positions they hold, and the duration with which they stay at the company." Further, though they aren't retiring, they do want some flexibility in their work, perhaps through decreased hours and part-time arrangements. They also want autonomy as they hold their decision-making skills and rationality in high regard. Baby boomers also value experience they typically equate with age and tenure within an organization and seek out respect and recognition for their knowledge and achievements.

Generation X is widely considered to be "self-reliant, hardworking…and fiscally responsible" and was "shaped by the evolution of personal computers" according to an uncredited article featured on Paychex.com. In the article titled "How to Manage the Five Generations in the Workplace," these workers were reported to be looking for work/life balance above all else. Primarily, Gen Xers want flexible work arrangements, childcare options that include working from home arrangements, and comprehensive rewards packages from their employers. This generation values benefits that include tuition reimbursement, stock options, and monetary gifts. This generation enjoys autonomy as well as psychological and physical space in their work environment. They're comfortable with communication via technology (e-mails, instant messages, etc.) and in person, both on the job and in the recruiting process.

Millennials—my generation—are the largest generation in the workforce with fifty-six million workers in 2019 per Great Place to Work's Managing Millennials Report. According to the report, Millennials are "far from being selfish job-hoppers; they're just searching for a position with great leaders, fair base pay, and support for their real-life needs." This support includes benefits such as student debt assistance and parental and eldercare leave. Millennials also value career advancement and professional development opportunities. Considering themselves a more "woke" generation, corporate social responsibility, diversity, equity and inclusion initiatives, and a feeling of purpose are also important to this generation.

Because we grew up in a time where the Internet transformed the world, we adapt easily to technology. We became accustomed to digital communications such as e-mail, instant messaging, and texting at a young age. Many millennials (my husband included) even *prefer* digital communications to anything in person or even a phone call. This makes virtual work very attractive for us. Oh, and don't hold us to that standard nine-to-five shift if there's no clear business need for it. We want flexibility and work/life balance. As long as we are getting results, many millennials don't see the point in being held to strict office hours.

Finally, we have Generation Z. Deloitte partnered with the Network of Executive Women (NEW) in 2018 to find out more about what this younger generation expects from employers for their "Welcome to Generation Z" report. The report put the findings into perspective. Generation Z was shaped by the Great Recession, where they saw their parents lose their jobs and millennial siblings move back home. This generation has also been affected by "rising nondiscretionary expenses, such as housing, transportation, food, and healthcare." It makes sense then that Generation Z is looking for "diverse and entrepreneurial opportunities with the safety of stable employment" while "prioritizing financial security over personal fulfillment." This means they may be more likely to remain loyal to a company and want longevity with their employer, but they expect fair pay.

This generation wants to work independently and "prefers individual tasks over team-based activities." Overall, much like millennials, this generation also wants work flexibility, career development opportunities, competitive pay, and a workplace with ethical practices. They value diversity and social impact and prefer to work for employers who share these values.

While what workers want is similar across generations, you can see, over time, company culture, work flexibility, management practices, and career development have become increasingly important. An employer's brand and social responsibility initiatives are considered when younger workers choose where to apply.

Now, of course, each individual is different, and these are generalizations of each generation's wants and needs in the workplace. Though this is based on research, I can attest to the accuracy based on my own observations and work within HR. Understanding these differences is important because as an HR professional, you need to be able to develop effective HR strategies and workplace policies that will work across each generation.

This all goes back to your strategies in talent acquisition and retention, total rewards, employee engagement, and performance management. The days where a worker expected only to receive a paycheck in exchange for their work have long been over. People are looking for much more from their employer and even the brands they support as consumers. Just think about yourself and what you want from an employer. Is a simple paycheck and basic benefits enough for you? Maybe, but wouldn't you *want* to work for an employer offering more of what you want, in an environment you can thrive in?

Simple data processing and administrative tasks being the core of what HR does is dead and gone. The time for strategic HR is here, now and in the future. The revolution in strategic thinking has already begun. If you're not already a part of it, you've got to catch up quickly.

THE WORSENING TALENT SHORTAGE

Over time, people strategies developed by HR have become increasingly important, especially when it comes to the war on talent. We've mentioned the "talent shortage" throughout this book and you're likely at least somewhat familiar with the talent shortage, or perhaps even fighting it now in your role. For anyone who isn't, the talent shortage is defined in simple terms by ManpowerGroup as "the disparity between what employers need and what available employees have to offer."

The 2020 ManpowerGroup research has shown the global talent shortage has almost doubled in the last decade, with businesses around the world (54 percent) reporting significant skill shortages and difficulties attracting talent in thirty-six of forty-four countries. US employers are reporting the most acute shortages at 69 percent.

This talent shortage has been around for a while, and it's only getting worse. Hence the phrase the "war on talent." Employers must become even more competitive when it comes to attracting and retaining the talent they need to operate and achieve business goals. Research conducted by Korn Ferry showed in their Future of Work report that by 2030, more than eighty-five million jobs could go unfilled because there aren't enough skilled people to take them. Per the report, "that talent shortage could result in about 8.5 trillion dollars in unrealized annual revenues." Yikes!

If you've been lucky enough not to feel this talent shortage now, get ready. We've seen lower birthrates for years, with the birthrate falling to its lowest level in thirty-five years since 1979, per the Centers for Disease Control and Prevention's Vital Statistics Rapid Release report on births provisional data for 2020. As workers retire and leave the workforce, we aren't having the same number of workers entering the workforce to replace them, which will make talent shortages even more intense in the next decade. In 2018, the World Economic Forum reported in their Future of Jobs Report that "54 percent of all employees will require significant reskilling and upskilling" in just three years.

Johnny C. Taylor, Jr., SHRM President and CEO, told me the talent shortage is one of the largest concerns for businesses and HR professionals. "We are going to have a serious war for talent. [We have] a birthrate problem, coupled with a skills gap problem, [and] an environment that demands higher skilled workers at a time when [due to the pandemic] we weren't able to educate the way we normally do. That's going to exacerbate the skills shortage. The number-one challenge, as we think strategically, is how we help our companies deal with this looming war for talent."

Scared yet? Maybe you should be, but this is one of the reasons why it is so imperative HR professionals act as strategic business partners now. We must work to be intentional and proactive in addressing the talent shortage through strategy. We must implement talent acquisition and retention strategies with training and development strategies that upskill and prepare your current workforce for the future.

As you can see, HR is responsible for so much more than paper processing, general administration, and planning parties. We've explored why HR is so critical in business, why business leaders and executives may not view HR as a strategic function, and why it's more important than ever before to be strategic within HR. In the following chapters, we'll dive into solutions to help HR practitioners become more strategic. This in turn helps business owners and leaders to see and understand the real strategic value of the HR function.

PART 3

FINDING SOLUTIONS

CHAPTER 9

The Right Focus and Mindset

"What you think, you become. What you feel, you attract. What you imagine, you create."

—BUDDHA

I have a question for you. As an HR professional, how do you view yourself? Do you see yourself as a major player in the business world? Do you see yourself as more of an individual contributor? Maybe you see yourself as the lonely HR representative no one wants to have lunch with because you're the fun police (I really hope that's not the case).

I've got another question for you. What do you focus on the most in your work? Compliance? Maybe recruiting? Perhaps it's any number of other HR responsibilities, all of which are deserving of our attention. I get it. Payroll must be processed, and it's got to be correct; no one ever wants to mess with an employee's pay.

Planning, coordinating, scheduling, and delivering training can be a beast. Providing guidance on a host of disciplinary issues that pop up takes time, and there's never-ending paperwork. Even if that paperwork is set up to be completed electronically, someone still has to take a look at it, ensure proper completion, approve it, etc.

It's so easy to become laser focused on these daily duties because they *are* important. Unfortunately, we can easily become trapped into a mindset related to these important tasks, where checking items off our list and being "productive" is all that matters. This sort of laser focus comes with blinders to other matters, such as strategic planning.

SEE YOURSELF IN A NEW LIGHT

What if I told you to be more strategic in HR, you could simply shift your mindset—the way you view yourself and what you focus on? It sounds crazy, right? It's so simple. But let me tell you, it works.

Years ago, one of my consulting clients in the healthcare industry (with several locations throughout the South) was so impressed with the results of the HR strategies I developed and implemented for them, they named me CHRO. This wasn't just a sweet little comment from someone saying, "Oh, we love you so much, we think of you as our chief human resources officer." No, this was listed within their company so all of their employees knew it. It was even included in their org charts.

Had I earned this designation through my consulting work? Absolutely. After conducting a comprehensive analysis of their business and their HR function, I put together effective strategies that helped this organization. Results included reduced turnover, increased employee engagement and productivity, and reduced risk through management training (among other things). I also focused on culture development within all of the strategies I implemented and I helped this employer position themselves for further growth. All of this had a positive impact on their bottom line, service to their patients, their overall reputation and brand, and their ability to open new locations.

My work had made such a positive impact that they wanted me present for all of their strategic planning activities and general leadership meetings. I was the leader for their HR function.

This client saw me as a business leader and claimed me as one of *their* business leaders. Prior to that, I hadn't seen myself that way. I thought of myself as a leader in HR, knew HR was critical for business success, and I knew my work was all in support of my client's business strategy. I just hadn't quite shifted my mindset to think of myself as a business leader. This client's elevation of my standing within their company was a lightbulb moment for me, and this was when it really clicked. *I am a business leader, not just an HR leader.*

It seems simple enough. HR is critical to business success, and HR strategies make an incredible impact on a business. The businesses' leaders are tasked with ensuring business success, *as is HR*. Therefore, HR is also a business leader!

HR takes a specialized approach to leading the business (the people) just as the finance executive does in finance, the marketing executive does in marketing, or the operations executive does in operations.

This shift to viewing HR professionals as business leaders isn't entirely new, though I needed an "aha" moment to see myself this way.

In an article for Gallup aptly titled "Why HR Leaders Never Become the CEO, but Should," Jeremie Brecheisen made a strong argument that HR leaders make great business leaders. For example, because of HR's people responsibility, he wrote they are able to "increase human capital returns during a merger and acquisition. Human capital becomes even more complicated during [the M&A] process." Brecheisen went on to point out how during this process, HR leadership is critical to ensure success. HR must help employees through change management, keep up morale, and maintain a positive employee experience as the culture is challenged.

Anyone who's been through a merger or acquisition knows it can be a delicate situation as employees become fearful, fatigued, and lose focus on the company's purpose.

Brecheisen continued, "This is a great area of opportunity for leaders because only 21 percent of people (in any given organization) believe their performance is managed in a way that motivates them to do outstanding work. It's not surprising that most companies struggle in this area when you consider that 82 percent of managers don't have the right kind of talent to manage people with true excellence." Brecheisen's argument highlights how HR is vital in helping a company hire and develop their talent, writing, "There is no one within the company more equipped to replace the broken practice of management than the people who've invested their careers in recruiting and supporting managers."

In mergers and acquisitions, HR is tasked in leading change management, culture acclimation and assimilation, and retention efforts. That's HR's role. It trickles down, of course, but would you put your CFO in charge of culture and change management? Probably not. These issues are the bread and butter of HR. Just look at the professional areas assessed in the Senior Professional in Human Resources (SPHR) certification from HRCI. Per the SPHR exam content outline, they include leadership and strategy, talent planning and acquisition, learning and development, total rewards, and employee relations and engagement. All of these elements are at play in mergers and acquisitions.

Brecheisen's argument doesn't stop there. He also wrote that HR leaders make great CEOs as "they can conquer agility by creating a culture of psychological safety and they can help their company build trust internally and externally."

MIND YOUR MINDSET
Bruce Waller is an esteemed HR professional and VP, Corporate Relocation of Armstrong Relocation and Companies. He is also an author, podcast host, and Texas SHRM board member. He recently spoke with me and revealed he takes the concept of HR professionals seeing themselves as business

leaders seriously. He views it as something important for HR professionals to be valued as a strategic partner.

Waller shared with me when he was studying for his HR certification years ago, he participated in a study group led by Barbara Hoover. "[Barbara] got up in front of the podium. The very first thing she said was the most important thing for HR is to know the business." This led Waller to reflect on his own career. He obtained his degree in business management and had worked in operations, then he went into sales and marketing before immersing himself in the HR community. "What I noticed is, for some reason, people kept referring to themselves as HR professionals. They are HR professionals, but they are business leaders. I think the mindset really needs to change [to include more than] 'I'm going to work in this company to [build] the HR competency.'"

Bruce touched on something that can be so key to helping HR professionals become strategic partners. If we shift our mindset from focusing solely on HR, or being an "HR leader" or an "HR expert," to thinking of ourselves as *business leaders*, naturally our focus will start shifting to that of the business as a whole. Once we are thinking this way and really focusing on the business overall, our HR strategies will be in support of the business strategy. We then become that HR strategist CEOs are looking for. Once we have assumed that role and it's visible to company executives from other departments, we've stopped perpetuating the idea HR isn't strategic in business.

Waller said to get that proverbial seat at the table where you are valued as a strategic partner, "You've got to learn the business, and you've got to know how does the business make money. Everybody knows the goals and the mission and things like that, but you've got to go *deeper* [and have] those conversations [about] how do we get customers, how do we make money, how do we do all of this."

HR is so critical to business success that HR strategies (or the lack of them) can make or break a business. Is this a bold claim? Sure, but I'm not saying it just because I love HR (which I do); just think of all the things HR is responsible for.

We hire people with the skills necessary to get the work done and lead our companies to success. HR implements and maintains competitive and well-managed total rewards packages that attract and retain top talent. In addition, we make sure workers are trained and developed throughout their tenure with the organization. We also work to ensure a positive experience is had by all of the workforce through cultivating company culture, providing career development opportunities, and ensuring employees remain engaged and productive at work. There's also compliance with a myriad of federal, state, and local laws and regulations. It's not fun, but we must keep up with compliance to prevent our companies from litigation, EEOC claims, costly penalties, etc.

This isn't even *everything* the HR team is doing.

HR is centered around people, but more importantly, HR is tasked with ensuring the people are driving the business forward. You can't make sure you've got the right people, in the right positions, doing the right things that will move the business forward, unless you *understand* the business. That means knowing all about the company, the industry, who your customers are, who your competitors are, what products and services the business is selling, etc.—basically, as Waller said, *how the business makes money*. If you don't know and understand this, you can't guide the people function in the right direction. To know and understand this, you must have business acumen.

We've really seen the agility and development of psychological safety and trust (both internally and externally) from HR professionals leading their organizations through the COVID-19 pandemic. It's also helped to create a shift in this viewpoint of HR professionals as business leaders. HR has led the charge in navigating the pandemic, employee safety, engagement, and more.

In their article, "Superhuman Resources: How HR Leaders Have Redefined Their C-Suite Role," David Reimer and Adam Bryant wrote about how HR has been placed center-stage during the pandemic, highlighting how HR has been responsible for employee safety during rapid changes in the way people work. These major changes came with new concerns, such as providing mental health support, finding new ways to measure performance, altering performance metrics, and employing new approaches to develop talent.

They also detailed how HR is a key player in answering questions surrounding company viewpoints on social movements like Black Lives Matter and driving the charge to ensure equity and inclusion. "All eyes in the room (or on videocalls) have turned to the chief human resources officer (CHRO) for the answers." While the circumstances of the pandemic and all it has brought are tragic, more HR leaders are being seen as business leaders than ever before. HR leaders are starting to view themselves as business leaders. This is an important step in becoming true strategic partners within a business and showing the value of the HR function as a strategic player.

INVEST THE TIME

Okay, let's be real. Just thinking of yourself as a business leader (you are!) isn't enough to be more strategic. It's helpful to shift your mindset, but I can think myself a llama all day long and it doesn't actually make me a llama. The next step in your mindset shift is to *make time for strategic thinking*.

Personally, I've made a habit (more of a ritual, really) of carving out time for strategic thinking throughout each day and week. As a business owner and HR consultant, I must have time for strategic thinking about my own business and those of my clients.

Each morning, for about half an hour, I start my day early with a cup of coffee on my balcony or porch (assuming it isn't raining) before I wake up my husband or kids. I sit in silence and think about my business. I think about where we are headed, what we need to do to get there, and what I'll be doing today to move the needle forward. I take simple notes so I won't forget any of my bright ideas (or anything else) and e-mail them to myself from my iPhone. This way, they will be waiting for me in my inbox.

Once I fire up my computer, I review my daily to-dos and get to work. Anytime I begin work on a client's project, task, etc., I take the time to consider their business goals and what can be done from an HR standpoint to achieve them. I consider this both for the right now and the long term. Then, I determine what I'll be doing to bring my clients a competitive advantage while addressing the projects and tasks at hand.

At least once a week, I schedule time to either write out my big ideas or talk them over with my husband. On particularly busy weeks, I find talking out my ideas is easiest, as I can tackle this after work while I'm cooking or doing laundry. As an added bonus, my husband typically ends up helping with these chores as he listens. It took time to get into this pattern, though. When I opened my consulting company, it was initially a one-woman show. I wore all the hats. Sales, marketing, accounting, etc. You name it, I did it. Fortunately, I built a book of business fairly quickly, so I provided my HR consulting services sooner than I had expected to. (I anticipated a much longer stint focusing solely on obtaining clients in the beginning.) However, that didn't take away everything else on my plate immediately, and I still had to keep prospecting, keep the books, and focus on strategy for HerrinHR and my clients.

While I now have a daily and weekly routine to focus on strategic thinking, it had to be developed over time. I began by first obtaining *The Mastery Journal* by John Lee Dumas. It's a journal that helps you focus and, per its subtitle, "master productivity, discipline, and focus in one hundred days." I primarily used this journal to schedule time for strategic thinking and hold myself accountable for it. In the journal, you create a morning routine and have four daily "sessions." You determine how much time you will devote to the session in "focus time" and how much time you have afterward for "refresh time." Then, you write out your focus for each session and jot down your accomplishments from the session once completed. Next, you rate yourself for each session based on your productivity and discipline (i.e., your ability not to be distracted).

There are a ton of other great aspects to this tool but using this really helped me determine *when* I could most effectively devote time to strategic thinking. This tool helped me recognize patterns and certain times of the day I would be more easily distracted when delving into this activity. It also helped me build the habit of taking time for strategic thinking.

As silly as making an appointment with yourself may feel at first, it's important.

In an article for the *Harvard Business Review* titled "Develop Strategic Thinkers Throughout Your Organization," Robert Kabacoff, VP of Research at Management Research Group (MRG), wrote about the importance of strategic thinking. Sharing the results of an unnamed follow-up study to a 2013 global study conducted by MRG on leadership practices and effectiveness, Kabacoff wrote, "When asked to select the leadership behaviors most critical to their organizations' future success, executives chose strategic 97 percent of the time."

Strategic behavior requires strategic thinking. In *The Strategic Thinking Manifesto*, research conducted by Rich Horwath, CEO of the Strategic Thinking Institute, showed 96 percent of five hundred leaders surveyed said they lacked the time for strategic thinking. So, if being strategic is the most important leadership behavior for an organization's success, but most leaders don't have the time for strategic thinking, it makes sense leaders should *make the time* and prioritize it. You don't even need to go on a fancy leadership retreat; simply block time off on your calendar and make sure you are respecting that time.

Dorie Clark, a marketing strategist who was named one of the top fifty business thinkers in the world by Thinkers50 in 2019, knows how important it is to take the time for strategic thinking. Feeling too overwhelmed to carve out time for this activity? Don't worry, Clark had a helpful tip to aid you in overcoming this. In a *Harvard Business Review* article titled "If Strategy Is So Important, Why Don't We Make Time for It?", Clark shared this advice, writing, "Even with limited time and the same amount of responsibilities, it's far easier to think strategically if you can clear the decks by doing simple things such as writing down all of your outstanding tasks in one place, so you can properly triage them and aren't constantly interrupted by the feeling that you forgot something."

Boom. Now you don't even have the excuse that you can block off time but won't be able to focus. Try Clark's approach, or whatever works for you, to have the mental space available for focusing on strategy. The bottom line is to make an appointment with yourself to think strategically.

Bruce Waller advocates for a mindset focused on strategic thinking in HR. During a recent conversation I had with him, he shared with me the importance of this focus during his time on the Board of Trustees for DallasHR. The Trustees' function was all about strategy, so it was incredibly important that they didn't get buried in the "weeds"—all that daily minutia that requires time and attention. The point of this is that while the "weeds" are important, when you're working in a strategic role specifically, you can't let that minutia take up all of your time.

Waller said, "How much time do you block out for just thinking? It's a small population [that does this]. I've asked a few people on my podcast that question, and David Windley (CEO of IQTalent Partners and SHRM Chairman of the Board) said blocking time [for this] is important." Since it's not an urgent task, our focus can (and often does) easily shift to urgent matters (that daily minutia). Then, at the end of the day, you find you skipped that appointment with yourself for strategic thinking. At that point, most of us just say, "Oh well, I'll get around to it next week." Blocking out time for strategic thinking, *actually making it an appointment on your calendar, and treating it as a priority even when you have other urgent tasks* can help HR leaders to stay focused on strategy and keep the right mindset.

FOCUS ON FUTURE GOALS

For many people, strategic thinking comes somewhat naturally in terms of achieving personal goals and advancing one's career.

For example, when I was younger and new to HR, I thought to myself, *What will it take for me to make it to the top? What education will I need? What experience should I get?* I thought about this and made action plans around it. I planned to take courses in human resources management and get an HR certification, and I planned to take jobs in specialty areas to get in-depth experience before moving on to any generalist or management roles. Then, I made it happen. These plans were my strategy.

This wasn't a one-time event either. I thought about my professional development and my career path frequently, over many years. I'm always working to get to the next level and thinking of my next steps. Occasionally I may let my mind wander to the far distant future and fantasize about being on major news stations discussing the world of work and HR. Delusions of grandeur? Perhaps. However, I see it as more of a BHAG (big hairy audacious goal) I plan to make happen.

It was easy for me to think strategically about my career moves and where I want to take my business. My mindset has always been to do more, be better, and get to the next level. That may not be your mindset but think about strategic thinking in terms of goal setting. When you're focused on a goal, it's natural to plan the steps to achieve that goal. Strategic thinking becomes a simple part of your planning process to achieve that goal.

I was recently speaking with a good friend of mine (who also happens to be my former boss), Anissa Wilson, about taking the time for strategic thinking. She shared with me this is an activity she indulges in when it comes to her own professional development and career moves. Wilson said, "I think about my personal goals [strategically]. I do a lot of planning and sit down at night and think, 'What's my next step? What do I have to do?'"

Strategic thinking about our professional careers is natural, but what about taking the time to think strategically at work about our organizations, moving them forward, and ensuring we are putting the right HR strategies in place?

Wilson works as an HR leader in the Professional Employer Organization (PEO) industry managing a team of HR consultants. Her work is extremely hectic and fast-paced, just as HR consulting outside of PEO is. "It's such a hair-on-fire environment; you have to put out the biggest fires first then move on to the smaller ones, every day." Although she has to work in such a frenzied environment, she is still a phenomenal strategic thinker. Not only must she be a strategic thinker as a leader in her own organization internally, but she must be a strategic thinker for clients as well. She also has to ensure her own team members are strategic partners for their clients too.

For Anissa, strategic thinking is something she has taken the time for both in and out of executive coaching sessions. Her executive coach worked with her to set goals and overcome the common obstacles many HR leaders face, such as obtaining buy-in from other executives and getting that "yes" on proposed strategies. This led to her thinking strategically about her team and her organization more often. This is a great approach, as she is able to use time set aside with her coach to think strategically.

For those who don't have access to an executive coach, I recommend asking a trusted colleague you admire to be your mentor. Be proactive in scheduling discussions and asking them questions. If you don't have access to an executive coach and you can't make calendaring time for strategic thinking work, you still have options. Make it a point to spend time on strategic thinking anytime you're in the car, a waiting room, the shower—you get my point.

To be a strategic partner in business, and to be a business leader, you must first be a strategic thinker. No more excuses; make the time!

CHAPTER 10

Overcoming the Skills Gap

―

"Once we accept our limits, we go beyond them."
—ALBERT EINSTEIN

I'm not much of a do-it-yourself crafting queen, I'm not handy with a glue gun, and when it comes to household projects and fixes, I'm even worse. You (and my husband) would never want me anywhere near broken plumbing or lighting fixtures, no matter how much I just want to help fix them. However, I am a big believer in continuous improvement—both within an organization and in terms of individual professional development. I'm not too shabby at that kind of DIY! That's why I am a big fan of the home improvement store Lowe's slogan, *Never Stop Improving*.

Throughout this book, we've covered what HR professionals need to do to improve, to step up their game and be seen as the strategic business leaders we really are (or should be, in some cases). We covered how important shifting your mindset is to make the transition into a strategic leader and thinker, and while that's important, simply shifting your focus alone may not be all you need to be an effective HR business partner or strategist.

As discussed in Chapter Five, many HR professionals have some skill gaps that, if left undeveloped, can impede their ability in strategic thinking. Each individual will have to spend some time reflecting to determine what those skill gaps are for themselves, as these skill gaps will vary from person to person. We all come from different backgrounds, experiences, and education, and this isn't anything to be ashamed of.

FILL IN THE GAPS

Everyone has an area (or two or five) in need of improvement. We're human. No one person is perfect in everything.

What matters here is what you do about it. Are you going to sit around and accept you have an area of weakness in the field, or are you going to do something about it? I'm not saying you need to become a master at everything HR. It's perfectly okay to have areas of strength, and some areas that are a little less easy or comfortable for you. When it comes to becoming a real strategic player in HR, it's definitely worth it to upskill yourself where it counts.

So how exactly do you determine what area may be a skill gap for you? Think about strategic thinking and planning and what part of that makes you uncomfortable. Is it forecasting?

Is it understanding or analyzing data and analytics, or putting them to practical use? How about understanding industry trends, or how the political, social, and economic landscapes affect your organization? Maybe you feel comfortable with all of that, but you get a little uncomfortable when it comes to knowing *how* to use all of that information. Is it difficult to anticipate and proactively address potential challenges? Maybe it's just understanding strategic thinking, or the strategic planning process as a whole.

When you find what makes you take pause and say to yourself, "You know, that's something I only know enough about to be dangerous," or think, *What does that even mean?*, you've found an area to develop your skills in.

If self-reflection of this sort is too uncomfortable to take part in, or if you have multiple areas to develop and aren't sure where to start, don't let yourself get overwhelmed. Don't give in to excuses and hold yourself back. Get out of your own way. You *can* conquer this mountain. The most important thing here is you try and you start. If you never start, you can't expect to improve. It's like learning to play and mastering an instrument. If you keep putting it off and telling yourself, "It's okay I didn't practice today, I'll just do it tomorrow," you soon find "tomorrow" never comes. The instrument remains dusty and unused in the corner, and the cycle repeats.

If you can't see the forest for the trees and need outside help to identify your areas in need of improvement, it's okay! I suggest finding a trusted colleague or mentor who can help. Someone who knows you well enough to provide you with this kind of input. Keep in mind, you want to pick someone who can deliver this kind of message in a way that won't make you feel like dirt. This colleague or mentor should want to see you succeed, not relish in an opportunity to break you down. (I mean, who wants that?) Also, make sure this is someone familiar with your role, responsibilities, and work so far. They need to understand what you're capable of now and your opportunities to improve.

This person should also be someone you share mutual respect with. Hearing you may need to work on a skill can be a hard pill to swallow, and this is especially true if they suggest you need to improve something you thought you were already decently skilled in. Again, we're all human, and sometimes hearing this is a hit to the ego, but just keep perspective. As Abhishek Ratna wrote in his book, *No Parking. No Halt. Success Non Stop!*, "A gap in skills and abilities reveal a golden opportunity!"

TALK TO THE BOSS

As I've shared previously, I've directly asked former bosses, "What do I need to do to get to the next level? Where can I improve?" That has helped me tremendously in determining not only my personal skills gaps, but also which skills gaps should be prioritized to reach my goals. This might be a great way for you to identify and prioritize what to work on too. Don't let this make you feel embarrassed; there is zero shame in self-improvement.

Are you afraid your boss might think less of you? Or are you concerned telling your boss you need help will backfire and hinder your chances for promotions or success? Worse, do you think going to your boss to ask for help will lead to a discovery that you're not as good as your boss thinks you are? Let me help you put those fears out of your mind.

As a business owner and people leader, I can tell you I *love* when employees take the initiative to improve themselves. If someone comes to me and asks me what they can do to improve their skills and asks me where they have a skills gap, it doesn't bother me in the slightest. I don't think to myself, *Oh, wow, I hadn't realized how much this person sucks in their work. They don't have the abilities I thought they did.* It's exactly the opposite. I want to champion those who seek to improve. I want to help them however I can. I think, *Wow! Good for you, taking the next steps to be the best you can be.* It shows me drive and ambition.

Paul Petrone wrote for the *LinkedIn Learning Blog*, "Most bosses want to help their employees grow, they want to be a mentor. This is because people both innately like helping other people where they can and because if you get better, they look better." That's true. Not only do humans generally enjoy helping others, but when an employee is a high performer, it reflects well on their manager. Petrone pointed out asking your boss how you can improve actually helps to develop your relationship with your boss. A good relationship with your boss is highly desirable. After all, they do have some influence over your pay, job tasks, and chances of promotion.

TAKE ACTION

So, whether you've self-determined your skill gaps or received help to identify them, the next step is to begin tackling them.

Create an action plan for yourself that includes the specific steps you'll take to improve your skills. Think about how you learn best and how deep of a dive you need to take. Traditional means of skill development you can explore include coursework, college programs, and classes. There are also webinars and seminars galore, books, podcasts, and even video tutorials online. If you're more of a hands-on learner, see if there are any workshops in your area and speak with coworkers in HR who can include you on activities and projects that will give you practical experience in the areas you wish to develop.

Know any HR consultants? Leverage those relationships and reach out! I—along with other HR consultants in my network—often find myself providing resources and guidance to other HR practitioners who want to grow. When I've had the time available, I've even put together mock scenarios and situations for others to work through. Once I even called an HR professional, put on a silly voice, and pretended to be from their management team. I relayed a fictitious scenario of a wayward employee to see how they'd walk through the issue. Roleplaying can be a little cringy at times, but not always, and it can be beneficial to see how you would respond to certain situations.

Don't have the time or resources for such activities? Never fear! There are absolutely simple things you can do to improve. Researching your industry and expanding your knowledge of the business you're in can help tremendously. When you understand all the moving parts that make the business work, you can more easily see the bigger picture.

Take the time to browse the Web and soak up what you can. Make a regular practice of reading news about your industry, your company, and your competitors from reliable sources (*The Onion* doesn't count). Treat your coworkers to coffee and pick their brains and remember you're not alone. There are many other HR professionals working on improving their skills who would be happy to do it right along with you. They aren't too hard to find either. You can join your local SHRM chapter to network with other HR professionals. You can even join an HR certification study group if certification is something you want to pursue. (Certification is something I highly recommend, by the way.)

Make a list of internal colleagues to speak with. Speak to a variety of people in different departments outside of HR to get a holistic perspective and understanding of how everything works together. These are simple activities that will help you have a broader understanding of your industry, company, and trends. If you're uncomfortable speaking with internal colleagues outside of HR, reach out to family and friends who work in other areas.

BETTER YOUR BUSINESS ACUMEN

As I've conducted research and interviews for this book, time and time again, I've received the same feedback. The most common skill leaders cite as "in need of development" among

HR professionals, what they consider to be holding them back from being strategic, is business acumen.

Business acumen, as you may remember from Chapter Five, is a more impressive way of saying business sense. It's all about your ability to understand and anticipate risks and opportunities, and how you handle them. It's about understanding how business works, being able to see the big picture, and coming up with effective means to achieve and improve business outcomes.

This year, I had the pleasure of speaking with Lee Cockerell. Cockerell is a former Executive Vice President of Operations for the Walt Disney World Resort (now retired), author of *Creating Magic: 10 Common Sense Leadership Strategies from a Life at Disney* (a book on management, leadership, and service excellence), and host of the *Creating Disney Magic* podcast. He's one of those renowned leaders who really *gets it*. He understands and values HR as a strategic function.

He told me during his time in leadership at Disney and Marriott, "HR was my right hand and finance was my left hand. You make those people your partners." He understood to drive customer satisfaction and financial performance within an organization, you have to hire the right people, train them right, and treat them right.

When we discussed HR strategy and what HR professionals can do to improve their strategic ability, Lee stressed the importance of brushing up on business acumen and taking up the simple task of reading the news. He said, "[It's about] looking at all kinds of data and information, and a wide range of what's going on in the world, so you can put that together to anticipate [what] could happen. Why should you know what the price of oil is and what's going on? Well, because it's going to affect your business." Cockerell spent his career in hospitality at Hilton, Marriott, and, of course, Disney, which we all know operates beloved resorts. He broke it down like this: The price of oil would affect those businesses because it will affect vacation travel and airfare through decreasing or increasing costs. That, in turn, would result in fluctuations in ticket sales as more or less patrons are able to travel. Those fluctuations have a direct impact on the financial performance of the business.

It might sound odd but reading the news to keep a pulse of the political, economic, social, technological, legal, and environmental landscapes (both domestically and internationally), will help you to predict business impacts. Those predictions are important. You need them to proactively design strategies to address these impacts. Doing your part to research your industry and regularly conducting a PESTLE analysis (PESTLE stands for political, economic, social, technological, legal, and environmental) will help you understand and anticipate business implications, which will help you to be a better strategic player.

I used to be one of those people who didn't read the news. I found it boring, depressing, or sometimes even frightening. Once I understood how what's going on in the world affects business, I made it a priority to read the news every day. I subscribe to various reputable publications that send daily recaps to my inbox (thanks, Business Journals!) and I have a few different news apps on my mobile device. I check these apps when I find myself with a few minutes between meetings or calls. My husband is also quite the news junkie himself and spends at least an hour each morning scouring his favorite news sources. He sends me anything he thinks I may find interesting too, and each night, at our dinner table, we discuss current events. We even include our kids in these talks—when the topics are age-appropriate, of course.

When I first realized I needed to improve my business acumen and strategic ability, and I began making a habit of reading the news, I made a game out of it. To see the bigger picture and better understand business implications, I would ask myself after each article I read, *How does this news affect my company?* I'd write down all the answers I could think of, then I would ask myself, *How does this affect our people?* I'd write down all the answers I came up with to that, too. Finally, I asked myself, *How can we best respond to or prevent this challenge?* If the impact to the business would be beneficial, I asked myself, *How can we take advantage of this opportunity and capitalize on it?* Then, you guessed it, I'd write those answers down.

Realistically, this was really hard at first, but it led me into further research and discussions about things I didn't have as solid a grasp on, things like supply chain logistics and aspects of technological capabilities outside of HRIS and payroll systems.

Cockerell said conducting your own research and staying on top of the news and what's generally going on out there in the world is vital. Cockerell shared it "all comes together to help you make better decisions. The more you know, the more you have, and at least you have a good shot at meeting the odds." In terms of taking the time (even in small increments) to develop your skills in any areas you have gaps, he said to think about "what should I be doing right now that may not pay off until later?"

It seems like such a simple thing, but it can make a big difference in your confidence and your strategic ability. No matter what it is you need to improve or how you go about it, the most important thing is to act. We don't reach our goals without action. We can't sit back and hope for knowledge to magically download into our brains. If you want to be a strategic business leader in HR, you must be a strategic thinker. To be a strategic thinker, you must first be intentional in your skill development.

What's the worst that can happen anyway? In just trying, you can make new connections, expand your knowledge, and gain confidence. It's totally worth the effort, and *you* are worth the effort.

CHAPTER 11

A Different Approach

"Failure is constructive feedback that tells you to try a different approach to accomplish what you want."

—IDOWU KOYENIKAN

Being a true strategic partner in HR means you have to bring some unpleasant information to your leadership team at times.

Personally, I had to deliver the findings of a sexual harassment investigation to a CEO that wasn't easy for him to hear; his top sales executive, and personal friend, was indeed harassing an employee. My recommendation was to let the sales executive go, which was quite a tough pill to swallow for the CEO, who was incredibly disappointed. However, as unpleasant as some news may be, your executives need to be aware of the people problems within your organization. They must also be kept aware of future challenges you need to proactively address. This is another reason why it's important to have that "seat at the table." You need your executive team's attention, trust, and respect so you can keep them abreast of people challenges within the business and obtain their support for the HR strategies you propose to help address these challenges.

Sometimes, working in HR, it can be difficult to get support from leadership on the strategies you wish to implement, even if you *do* have that seat at the table. It's not always easy to get a CEO or another member of the C-suite to sign off on what you're proposing. Maybe they don't like something within the strategy you've created, maybe they don't see the value in it, or maybe they think it's going to be too cumbersome or costly to implement. Perhaps they might even think it's just not an important issue because they're more focused on product development or an acquisition. Our role as HR leaders is really to provide the executive team with the education and the background that they need to understand the importance of the issue you're trying to solve.

PROVIDE OPTIONS AND EDUCATION FOR EXECUTIVE BUY-IN

If they don't like what they're hearing (maybe it's some sort of unpleasant information), we have to explain why action must be taken. We must make clear how the company may be at risk. In addition, we must convince our leaders why our proposed actions are the company's best bet moving forward, as tempting as it may be to just ignore the issue entirely. We can't leave it up to the C-suite to figure it out on their own. Certainly, some executives are able to do that, but it's incumbent on us as HR professionals to offer that education as part of the entire package. This is just one step in helping them understand and appreciate the value in the strategy you are proposing.

I was recently speaking with Mark Brown, a human resources officer at the Department of Defense, about what it takes to get that "yes" (that support) from executives. Most of us have heard before if you're going to bring up a problem, you need to prepare a solution to bring with it. Having a solution to the problem at the ready helps to prevent the perception that you're just a complainer. However, even though proposing a strategic solution certainly isn't complaining, a lot of HR professionals still struggle with getting executive buy in.

I was curious about Brown's experience and how he ensures he gets the "yes" on what he's proposing, or at least how he gets a "yes" more often than he gets a "no." He shared with me something I absolutely love and think all HR professionals can find valuable. When presenting a problem to leadership, he provides the background to the issue and takes things a step further. He provides multiple solutions to his leadership team. Brown said, "I'm coming in with three options and I'm going to give a recommended option."

This is something he learned during his time in the military. These three strategy options are called Courses of Action. Each Course of Action is a fully thought-out strategy, not just an idea. When presenting the three different options, he walks the leadership team through each option, explains what they can reasonably expect as the result of each option (both the good and the bad), and then provides his own recommendation as to which of the three options would be best and why. Finally, he leaves it up to the leaders to select the strategy they wish to proceed with.

Mark told me using this method results in his leadership team selecting his recommended strategy 90 percent of the time or more. Occasionally, they might like elements of each of the three strategies and request he put a new strategy together that combines these elements. Alternatively, his leaders may select a single strategy but request a few tweaks to it. Either way, his method works to proactively avoid a complete "no" to his proposals. Since his options are thought out and all are viable, it's less likely he will receive an outright "no." This way, Brown doesn't have to go back to the drawing board and he's providing value to his leadership team.

This method of presenting three strategies for selection also demonstrates he is service-oriented to the people in the organization and the leadership team, as he is willing to go the extra mile and design multiple solutions.

BECOME AN INTERNAL CONSULTANT
This reminds me of consultative leadership. In a 6Q blog, Gerald Ainomugisha perfectly defined this leadership style, writing, "Consultative leadership entails asking key people for their thoughts and allowing them time to process the problem and solve for what they feel was the best possible solution." Consultative leadership is about the ability to influence others rather than telling them what to do while imposing your authority on them. When we are able to include others in the decision-making process, we receive more buy-in. Our executives are naturally going to be much more inclined

to accept what we're presenting when they have a hand in choosing the solution. Like my mother always said, you can catch more flies with honey than you can with vinegar.

I find this to be a phenomenal approach in my own practice as an external HR consultant, and I do the same thing Brown does. I will explain a current issue to my client, or a potential challenge we need to be proactive in addressing (education and background), then I will provide my client with a few different strategies to solve the problem (Courses of Action) whenever possible. I also go over the anticipated results of implementing each of these options, as well as the option I recommend (consultation). Generally speaking, 90 percent of the time or more, my clients select the option I have recommended too.

When speaking with Brown, I began wondering if I'd ever taken this kind of approach prior to becoming an external HR consultant. To be totally honest, when I reflected on this, I realized it's not something I had consciously thought of. I did brainstorm for potential solutions to problems with colleagues and superiors in the past, but overall, I didn't *really* formally present more than one solution or strategy at a time. As a result, I had to go back to square one (the frustration was real) to think of a solution that would work for our leadership team far too often.

I think reasons for this can be attributed to my desire to be seen as someone with the singular, definitive answer to a problem. This was when I had executives with a narrow view of my role within HR. Combined with that view, at the time, I didn't think of broader business implications, and our leaders had a very autocratic style of management, which was wholly ineffective for me.

It's natural and easy for me to utilize Brown's method of presenting multiple strategies as an external consultant. I'm sharing this approach because I realize I could have been much more successful as an internal HR leader earlier in my career if I had thought of this and made use of it. Brown learned this method during his time in the military but has since taken this with him everywhere he's gone to work and it's provided him with much success.

In addition to boldly asking your executive team what they want and are looking for in terms of your HR work, using this consultative approach will serve your mission to become a strategic business leader. As you inform your leaders of what the people of your organization want and need, provide background and education, and multiple strategies for selection, you position yourself as a strategic thinker. The more you are seen as a strategic thinker, the easier it becomes for executives to see you as an effective strategic business partner. Over time, this highly influential consultative approach will likely get you that "yes" more often. The more often you get that "yes," the more often you get to have (and keep) your seat at the table.

DEVELOP RELATIONSHIPS
Building relationships with your leadership team is going to be incredibly important when you're trying to take a consultative approach and be a strategic partner. You can come up with strategies and options and pitch them until you're blue

in the face, but without some level of trust and respect, they can easily be shot down. Just as it's important to build relationships with the employees we serve in HR, it's important to develop relationships with your leaders.

I was able to speak with Tammy Duncan, the Executive Vice President of HR at Lamar, the nation's leading outdoor advertising company, on this idea. We were discussing being strategic in HR, and she spoke to the importance of developing relationships with your C-suite. "I really think the biggest thing that's been helpful to me [in] reporting directly to the CEO...was building that relationship slowly over time. You can't hit people over the head with your idea; you have to gradually get them to trust you." She said (and I agree) so much of what we do within HR centers on trust.

Duncan then shared her favorite leadership quote with me from Harry Truman: "Leadership is the ability to get [people] to do what they don't want to do and like it." For Duncan, this means building relationships to draw people in and earn their trust. The more they trust her, the more they will listen and allow her to lead them down the right path. If we want to show our value as a strategic partner, it isn't enough to deliver strategy in addition to handling administrative and tactical aspects of our role. We must go beyond that and also consistently build relationships and trust with those in our organization. That trust helps others to follow us, even if it's something they don't necessarily want to do.

THE OUTSOURCING ADVANTAGE

Finally, I would be remiss not to tell you about the benefits of HR outsourcing. HR consultants, like myself, use a consultative approach with clients, just as Brown does within his organization internally. This is another great tool you can utilize to ensure you are able to be strategic in HR. Don't be alarmed. I know, after reading everything I've presented so far about how critical the HR function is, you may be wondering why on earth I would possibly recommend outsourcing this super critical function. Wouldn't it be better to keep all HR duties in house?

I understand the trepidation some may have when it comes to HR outsourcing, but there are a host of benefits to be realized when you take this approach. Let's first take a look at the delegation opportunities it provides an internal HR professional.

I've made a case for scheduling strategic thinking and shifting your focus to strategic initiatives. The reality is for many, especially those operating as an HR department of one, there isn't a lot of actual time to do this. Daily "fires" (those emergencies or urgent issues that seem to spring up at random) easily prevent that focus shift to the strategic. While you are building your ability to carve out time for thinking, why not delegate administrative HR functions through outsourcing?

Engaging a competent HR consultant you can trust, or even an HRO (Human Resources Outsourcing), ASO (Administrative Services Outsourcing), or PEO (Professional Employer Organization) firm, to take on regular administrative tasks can free up a massive amount of time for you. Just think about payroll alone; how much time do you devote to payroll processing tasks each pay period? Is it several hours? A day or more? What about researching compliance guidance for all of the questions that come up around all those employment law acronyms like FMLA, ADA, PDA, VEVRAA, etc.? Not to mention the time it takes to do things like write and revise your employee handbook and job descriptions (which ideally should be updated at least annually). How about the time it takes to recruit new talent or investigate a claim of sexual harassment or discrimination?

Using an HR consultant or HRO (or other such outsourcing vendor) allows you to get these tasks off your plate. Sure, you'll still need to take care of those "fires," but you'll have time left over for strategic thinking, planning, and actually taking action. Your consultant can even help you navigate those fires more quickly and easily, too! Part of my job as a consultant is to provide answers and guidance on compliance questions and general questions about how to handle unique situations with employees. Don't waste time spinning your wheels or worse, googling how to handle whatever scenario you're faced with. Instead, call your consultant for help!

Outsourcing HR tasks and using an HR consultant can give you great peace of mind while mitigating your risk. Dinsmore Steele, a PEO broker, wrote on their website the two most significant reasons a business uses an HR outsourcing service (a PEO, for example) are the time management benefits it provides and the protection it provides. Per their site, "When it comes to human resources issues, claiming naivete isn't going to get a business owner off the hook for penalties or legal action. By hiring an expert in payroll, benefits, or any number of human resources tasks, the small business owner is transferring the risk to them to handle it legally."

The experts you outsource to can provide compliance guidance and, in many cases, may even inform you of laws or requirements you didn't know about that apply to your business or situations you're faced with. In some instances, such as in investigations, it's better to let an expert third party handle things for you. It's hard to argue the findings of an unbiased third party, after all. That outside third party doesn't have a stake in the outcome and isn't involved in your office politics.

Outsourcing HR to a reputable HRO vendor also provides you with some great tech, which may be comparable to or better than what you're already using internally. HR technology provides another means to save time via automation. A state-of-the-art human resources information system (HRIS) that handles it all is worth the investment. Most handle timekeeping, payroll, benefits administration, performance management, learning management, company property tracking, and more. These systems house and help you to manage employee data while providing you with reporting features and data and analytics tools. These systems are a massive help to you in HR when it comes to saving time on paper processes and having tools and data at your fingertips to make effective HR strategies.

Additionally, this kind of technology is what employees of today have come to expect. Think of all your paper processes. These might include new hire onboarding, benefits enrollment, time off requests and PTO tracking, performance management, and more. Paper processes for these are a thing of the past, not to mention environmentally unfriendly. As LBMC Employment Partners wrote in their blog, "Outsourcing can improve employee relations and streamline hiring orientation." That's right, you can make a better first impression with your new hire orientation through an HRO's HRIS technology. HROResources.com shared on their website that "employees expect their work experience to be as seamless and technology-friendly as their personal consumer experience…Employers have been forced to ensure that their HR technology stack provides an integrated and seamless employee experience."

Let's flip this around a bit. It's clear using an HR consultant or HRO can provide some amazing benefits, including putting time back on your plate to focus on strategies that move the needle forward in your business. But what about the HR professionals who don't have that problem? Perhaps you have the time but are still working to upskill yourself in data and analytics, business acumen, forecasting, or even just strategic thinking itself. Using an HR consultant or HRO can be a brilliant move for anyone who finds themselves in such a situation.

Again, you're outsourcing to experts, so why not let them handle strategy development for you? This is something I handle for clients regularly. For some clients without an HR presence internally, or for those I'm a fractional HR leader for, I'm solely responsible for HR strategy. For other clients with an HR representative, I may consult in a particular focus area. These run the gamut and include diversity, equity, and inclusion (DE&I), talent acquisition, and total rewards, among other areas. Any one of these may be an area my client's internal HR representative(s) aren't as experienced in, and they feel more comfortable having an expert take it on.

Other times, it could be the client has another major project to work on and they trust me to take care of this strategy development for them. This ensures their focus isn't pulled away from their project prematurely. After all, as a consultant, I make it my business to learn all about my client's business. I've found this to be effective for many organizations, as I'm able to take a holistic view as an unbiased outsider and create effective strategies while still considering the ins and outs of my client's organizations—internal politics included, when necessary.

As an example, a few years ago, a client of mine (a wealth management firm) was in a high growth phase, and every employee was strapped for bandwidth. They had a new-to-HR internal representative I was working with who was lovely but very green. So, when an employee of theirs disclosed they wanted to come out at work as trans and present as a female, that green HR employee turned to me. My client was happy to have me take the reins, as this was unfamiliar territory that came with a host of questions. What laws did they need to comply with? How did they need to navigate this in a way that made the employee feel safe and comfortable? Did they need to provide a separate bathroom space? How would they communicate this to the rest of the team and their clients? How could they enforce team members using the proper pronouns?

I'm proud to say my client never once made a derogatory remark about the employee who was bravely sharing their journey with their peers. My client truly wanted to make certain she felt safe, supported, and included. I was able to answer all of my client's questions and ensure they remained compliant with all applicable laws. Most importantly, I was able to provide strategies surrounding diversity, equity, and inclusion that worked for their business and their employee's journey. It was a great success, and the employee received a fantastic welcoming when she came to the office as her authentic self. The client's internal HR representative was also able to learn quite a bit, as I kept her abreast of everything I was doing. I gave her the education she needed to understand the *why* behind all of my recommendations.

That's another great benefit of using an HR consultant. You can learn a phenomenal amount as you ask questions and receive deliverables you've tasked to the consultant. I am a big proponent of education, and one thing I do with all of my clients is provide them with as much information as I can (and that they want) surrounding my guidance, recommendations, and strategies. This has been tremendously helpful to HR professionals I work with, as well as those primary contacts I have with clients who don't have an internal HR employee.

Whether you are looking to generate some time savings through automation and streamlining HR tasks through HRO technology or you are interested in HR consulting so you can focus on strategy, outsourcing can be a wise investment. Be the hero and move things forward for your organization by having an expert develop strategy either for or with you as you upskill yourself. Put your energy back toward a major project while you leave the rest to HR experts. The benefits of engaging an HR consultant or HRO are undeniable as another great method to help you become more strategic in your role.

Conclusion

"Every action has an impact; choose wisely the impact you want to have."

—MINDY HALL

HR's role in an organization is a powerful one. *People* make or break a business, p*eople* drive a nonprofit organization's mission, and p*eople* are responsible for it all. They create the products and provide the services companies deliver. Without the people, we have nothing.

HR is the shepherd of both the people and the company, delicately balancing employee and employer needs. Human resources should be taken seriously and shouldn't be an afterthought. Waiting to have an HR presence until reaching an arbitrary number of employees is unwise, while relegating an HR professional to administrative tasks alone is detrimental to business success.

Someone needs to bring the right people in the door and put them in jobs where they can truly contribute the best of their skills. Someone needs to push for employee training, development, and continuous improvement while ensuring performance is managed well and fairly. Someone must be responsible for looking to the future of the organization and how its people will take it there. Someone must ensure regulatory compliance and mitigate risk. Someone must do all of this while simultaneously anticipating future needs and challenges and proactively creating appropriate strategies.

That someone is in HR.

It's the HR professionals who move a business forward through people strategies. You need to develop a new product that will shake up the market? HR will find the people to create it, market it, and sell it. You need to keep internal knowledge held by your rock star employees? HR will create the retention strategies necessary to make that happen. You want to build your employer brand and have a great place to work? HR will take that on with total rewards and culture strategies.

HR is capable of so much more than we are often given credit for. HR deserves a seat at the table, and to get it, we have to prove we are strategic thinkers. If we lack strategic thinking ability, we can't act as strategic partners.

When we take the time to think strategically, improve our skills so our gaps are transformed from areas of weakness to areas of strength, build our relationships with executives, and demonstrate our business acumen, we can prove we aren't just paper-pushers. We in HR are business leaders. We are people leaders, and we can change the world.

Due to the nature of our role, HR professionals have an opportunity to create better workplaces and change lives for the better. We can help design the future of work as we know it by fighting for living wages and ethical work practices, and we can push for true equity and inclusion for all. To do these things, we must be heard, we must be valued as strategic partners, and we must be trusted advisors.

These are the reasons I love HR so much. HR makes a big impact. The right job, in the right environment, is powerful. There was a time, when I was a teenager, I was without stable housing and on my own. I didn't expect to amount to much, despite my nearly 4.0 GPA in high school. During my time in high school, I knew I wanted to go places and be somebody, so I worked hard. I was an officer in my school's National Honor Society and involved in a myriad of extracurricular activities. I even lettered in academics and upon graduation, I was a Texas Scholar!

Circumstances beyond my control resulted in the situation I was faced with, and my dreams of going to college right after high school were dashed. Instead, my time was spent working whenever I could and finding couches to crash on so I wouldn't have to sleep in my car. It wasn't easy, and I'll admit, after a while, I fell into some bad habits that didn't serve me well. I was tired of just trying to survive; I felt like my life had no meaning or hope. Still, I kept on.

Tired of working for minimum wage, I applied for a different job. Yeah, I'd only be making eleven dollars an hour at this new company, but what an increase! I was offered the position and happily took it.

When I took that job, I had an epiphany. It was a small moment in time, but it changed the course of my life. I thought, *This is my chance to make it. This is my chance to do something with my life, to get out of here. I can turn away from the things that don't serve me and put my all into this. It has to be better than what I have now, which is just shy of nothing.*

Having that job gave me dignity. It made me feel like somebody. I was part of a close-knit team, I felt valued, and I was given opportunities to develop my skills. I worked my ass off and the owner of the company began paying for me to go to college at night. I felt good about myself because I was set up to be successful, and I *was* successful. I did a great job, received several promotions over time, and my confidence grew along with my capabilities. My personal situation improved dramatically. I now had my own place, and I found connection and belonging at work.

From there, I've continued to work hard. I've come a long way; I now have my own company and I'm fulfilled professionally. In my personal life, I live in my dream house with my amazing husband and two wonderful children. I know firsthand the power of a job. I understand the impact made on an individual when they are set up for success in the right position. I know the difference company culture makes on a work environment and how that work environment can be a force for positive change.

This is why I love HR. Not only can we drive business forward, but we have such an amazing opportunity to drive positive change in the workplace, too. When we have a seat at the table, there is so much we can do. We can remove barriers to employment for the marginalized, we can keep workers safe, and we can create environments that build people up and bring them together.

HR has heard we should be strategic partners for years, but we still aren't all there yet. I had to go on my own journey to become a strategic business leader, and it took years. I've shared that frustration in not being heard by executives and I know what it's like for HR to be treated as only a tactical function. My hope is this book will help you in your journey to be a strategic thinker and business leader in HR.

HR is having a moment. Seize it! Don't let this opportunity pass you by. Business owners and executives turned to HR professionals for advisement throughout the COVID-19 pandemic, they've turned to us to fight the war for talent, and they've turned to us to guide them on diversity, equity, and inclusion. This is our time to take our work in HR to the next level. This is our time to demonstrate the HR function is a strategic one so we earn and keep our seat at the table.

Join the strategic thinking revolution and be *intentional* in HR.

Acknowledgments

This book wouldn't have been possible without the amazing people who contributed their time, wisdom, and support to the endeavor. Writing my first book hasn't been a walk in the park, but those who were by my side throughout the journey have made it infinitely easier than it would have been without them. Truly, this book wouldn't have become a reality without you all, and I am incredibly grateful to you.

First, to my husband, James, I cannot say thank you enough for everything you've done for me. In addition to being my biggest supporter and always encouraging me to go after my dreams, you have done everything you could to allow me time and space to write this book. You've seen my many emotional states throughout this process and met me wherever I needed you. When I was excited, you celebrated with me. When I was frustrated and tired, you gave me the motivation to continue. When I fell apart, cried, and thought I couldn't do it, you reminded me of who I am and that I could. When I was proud of myself for accomplishing this goal, you were prouder. You always keep me looking to the future with you. You're my hero. I love you.

Second, I'd like to thank my children, Jenna and Nathan. You both are the reason I work so hard and why I will never settle for anything less than absolute excellence. I am so proud of both of you and I love you more than anything.

Next, I'd like to thank my friends who have continued to check in on me and offer words of encouragement. My friends are some of the best people around and I'm so glad to have you all in my life.

Thank you to my dad, who instilled in me a love of reading and writing as a child. Thank you to my mom, who inspired me to work hard to have the life I've always dreamed of. Thank you also to my sister, Amber, and my brother, Rider, for being some of the greatest humans ever.

To each and every individual I interviewed while conducting research for this book, I admire you all immensely. I cannot thank you enough for your generosity of time and insight. Your wisdom has made this book come to life and I am truly grateful you agreed to contribute to this project.

I would be remiss not to thank two of the best bosses I've ever had. Allison Johnson, thank you for pushing me to pay attention to all the details and think about the bigger picture. Anissa Wilson, thank you for being the kind and brilliant leader you are.

To the team at New Degree Press, and most especially editors Quinn Karrenbauer and Michelle Pollack, thank you so much for all of your hard work and support. As you know, there were plenty of days I felt overwhelmed and thought I couldn't do it, but you lifted me up and got me to the finish line.

Finally, thank you so much to all who preordered this book and made its publishing possible:

Butch Bagley
Penney Bagley
Shannon Barrett
Lindsay Becker
Renee Bertalan
Sid Blache
Norma Brito
Mark Brown
Fabia Bourda
Keenon Bushnell
Amy Carnes
Joshua Carney
Randy Cazarez
Danny Cisneros
Carolyn Clungston
Amy Cook
Marquee Crandall
Rachel Deitz
Courtney DeWitt
Demetria Diggles
Tammy Duncan-Swope
Mark Franklin
Miranda Gardner
Tameka Gormer
Lyne Gress Register
Joseph Guerrero

Xavier Gutierrez
John Hagan
Paul Hagerty
Chris Herrin
Renee Herrin
Dunreeth Jahnsen Cole
Summer Jelinek
Allison Johnson
Sergey Kochergan
Tiffany Kromer
Rheann Leech
Donna Meek
Jenny Moore
Melissa Moore
Whitney Mundt
Natalie Nicodemus
Kenneth Orr
Aaron Pratt
Michael Raley
Drew Reynolds
Emma Riley
Debbie Romeyn
Ashley Ruiz
Jason Sandler
Thomas Schmitt
Brandi Sewell-Jones

Amber Shultz
Mark Sinatra
David Stephenson
Tiffany Stevenson
Denise Stewart
Glynnis Swan
Heidi Torres
Cyndi Tuttle
Georgina Ty
Bruce Waller
J. Lea Weaver
Kristi Welch
Michele Williams
Anissa Wilson

Appendix

INTRODUCTION

Guarino, Alan and Jim Newfrock. *The CEO's HR Imperative.* Korn Ferry, 2018.

Merriam-Webster. "Intentional. Definition of Intentional." Accessed October 2, 2021. https://www.merriam-webster.com/dictionary/intentional#:~:text=1%20%3A%20done%20by%20intention%20or,Sentences%20Learn%20More%20About%20intentional.

Merriam-Webster. "Revolution. Definition of Revolution." Accessed October 2, 2021. https://www.merriam-webster.com/dictionary/revolution.

Morgan, Jacob. *The Employee Experience Advantage.* Wiley, 2017.

State of the American Workplace. Washington: Gallup, 2017. https://www.gallup.com/workplace/238085/state-american-workplace-report-2017.aspx.

CHAPTER 1

Goodreads. "Starting Quotes. (59 quotes)." Accessed October 2, 2021. https://www.goodreads.com/quotes/tag/starting.

CHAPTER 2

Barney, Jay. "Firm Resources and Sustained Competitive Advantage." *Journal of Management* 17, no. 1 (March 1991): 99–120. https://doi.org/10.1177/014920639101700108.

BrainyQuote. "The ground beneath you is shifting, and…" Accessed October 2, 2021. https://www.brainyquote.com/quotes/bonnie_hammer_853313?src=t_shifting.

Gallup. "CliftonStrengths Online Talent Assessment." Accessed August 5, 2020. https://www.gallup.com/cliftonstrengths/en/252137/home.aspx?utm_source=google&utm_medium=cpc&utm_campaign=us_strengths_branded_cs_ecom&utm_term=gallup%20strengths%20finder&gclid=CjwKCAjwhuCKBhADEiwA1HegObuUYGWjZOKOuHgYqoWqrg8qGZbKSb2ocwkuUCuiamMfOsIMXwSbcBoClocQAvD_BwE.

Human Resources Certification Institute. "Is this Certification Right for Me?" Accessed May 19, 2021. https://www.hrci.org/our-programs/our-certifications/phr.

Huselid, Mark A. "The Impact Of Human Resource Management Practices On Turnover, Productivity, And Corporate Financial Performance." *Academy of Management Journal* 38, no. 3 (1995): 635–672. https://doi.org/10.5465/256741.

Ulrich, Dave. *Human Resource Champions: The Next Agenda for Adding Value and Delivering Results.* Boston: Harvard Business School Press, 1997.

HRD.tv. "What's the Role of HR in Strategic Thinking." December 9, 2015. Video, 3:21. https://www.youtube.com/watch?v=lablFadnBCY&list=PLMJ9rvpCbsYr3A5hsw5_WpHzerVGo6IY_&index=7.

CHAPTER 3

ABC News. "True Confessions: Ex-HR Exec Tells All." April 28, 2012. Video, 6:09. https://www.youtube.com/watch?v=zBIjVXHl1aA&t=1s.

Armin Trost. "#01 The Strategic Side of Human Resources Management." March 28, 2020. Video, 33:12. https://www.youtube.com/watch?v=x3TmoJfHu4k&list=PLMJ9rvpCbsYr3A5hsw5_WpHzerVGo6IY_&index=2.

The Balance Careers, Susan Heathfield. "Reasons Why Employees Hate HR." Accessed June 24, 2021. https://www.thebalancecareers.com/reasons-why-employees-hate-hr-1917590.

BrainyQuote. "Marcus Aurelius—Nothing has such power to broaden the…" Accessed October 2, 2021. https://www.brainyquote.com/quotes/marcus_aurelius_118558?src=t_broaden.

Crowley, John. "Are All HR Professionals Incompetent?" *HR Insights Blog.* May 29, 2019. https://www.peoplehr.com/blog/2019/05/29/are-all-hr-professionals-incompetent/.

Human Resource Management. Minneapolis, 2016.

Johnson, Phil. "HRM in Changing Organizational Contexts." In Human Resource Management: A Critical Introduction, edited by David G. Collings and Geoffrey Wood, 19–37. London: Routledge, 2009.

Reed, Sandra. PHR® and SPRH® Professional In Human Resources Certification Complete Study Guide. Indianapolis: Sybex, 2019.

Vinay Kumar S. "The Historical Background of Human Resource Management." Article. Published on October 12, 2015. https://www.linkedin.com/pulse/historical-background-human-resource-management-vinaykumar-s/.

CHAPTER 4

Goodreads. "Becoming Who You Re Meant To Be (16 Quotes)." Accessed October 2, 2012. https://www.goodreads.com/quotes/tag/becoming-who-you-re-meant-to-be.

Holley, Nick. What CEOs Want From HR. Henley Business School, 2014.

Korn Ferry. "HR Heal Thyself' Korn Ferry CHRO Survey Reveals Serious Gaps in HR Talent Including Low Business IQ." Accessed May 5, 2021. https://www.kornferry-dev.com/content/kornferry/en/about-us/press/hr-heal-thyself-korn-ferry-chro-survey-reveals-serious-gaps-in-hr-talent-including-low-business-iq.html.

Lee, Tony and Dana Wilkie. "How HR Can Earn the CEO's Trust." *HR Magazine*, November/December 2018. https://www.shrm.org/hr-today/news/hr-magazine/1118/Pages/how-hr-can-earn-the-ceos-trust.aspx.

Sinar, Evan, Rebecca Ray, Richard Wellins, Stephanie Neal, Adam Canwell, Amy Lui Abel, Amanda Popiela, Joe Dettman, Louise Rolland, Liz Collins, and Tony Cotton. *Global Leadership Forecast 2018: 25 Research Insights to Fuel Your People Strategy*. Development Dimensions International, Inc., The Conference Board Inc, and EYGM Limited, 2018.

CHAPTER 5

AZ Quotes. "Top 25 Asking Why Quotes (of 54). Accessed October 2, 2021. https://www.azquotes.com/quotes/topics/asking-why.html.

Biro, Meghan. Viser. "Why HR Data is the Key to Strategic Business Decisions." Accessed June 1, 2021. https://www.visier.com/clarity/why-data-is-the-key-to-strategic-hr-decisions/.

CAHRS Working Groups. *State of HR Analytics: Facts and Findings from CAHRS Topical Working Groups*. Cornell University ILR School, est. 2011.

Collins, Laurence, Dave Fineman, and Akio Tsuchida. *Rewriting the Rules for the Digital Age: 2017 Deloitte Global Human Capital Trends*. Deloitte University Press, 2017.

Cope, Kevin. *Seeing the Big Picture: Business Acumen to Build Your Credibility, Career, and Company.* Austin: Greenleaf Book Group Press, 2012.

Indeed Career Guide. "Business Acumen Skills: Definition and Examples." Accessed September 10, 2021. https://www.indeed.com/career-advice/career-development/business-acumen-skills.

Levenson, Alec and Gillian Pillans. *Strategic Workforce Analytics.* London: Corporate Research Forum, November 2017.

Summerfield, Brian. "A Crisis in Leadership" Archived June 23, 2009, at the Wayback Machine, Chief Learning Officer Magazine, April 2008.

Van Vulpen, Erik. "The Impact of People Analytics and the Growing Skills Gap." *LinkedIn.* March 19, 2019. https://www.linkedin.com/pulse/impact-people-analytics-growing-skills-gap-erik-van-vulpen/.

Volini, Erica, Jeff Schwartz, Brad Denny, David Mallon, Yves Van Durme, Maren Hauptmann, Ramona Yan, and Shannon Poynton. *The Social Enterprise at Work: Paradox as a Path Forward, 2020 Deloitte Global Human Capital Trends.* Deloitte Insights, 2020.

CHAPTER 6

Altman, Jack. *People Strategy: How to Invest in People and Make Culture Your Competitive Advantage.* Hoboken: John Wiley & Sons, Inc., 2021.

Ashish. "An Employee-Centric Organization is Indeed a Business-Centric Organization." *TheCultureTimes (blog)*. August 20, 2019. https://culturro.com/blog/2019/08/20/an-employee-centric-organization-is-indeed-a-business-centric-organization/.

BrainyQuote. "Judy Smith—there's always an opportunity with crisis..." Accessed October 2, 2021. https://www.brainyquote.com/quotes/judy_smith_823185.

Business.com. "Creating an Employee-Centric Company Culture Will Not Be the Death of Your Business." Accessed June 4, 2021. https://www.business.com/articles/creating-an-employee-centric-company-culture-will-not-be-the-death-of-your-business/.

Gallup. McFeely, Shane and Ben Wigert. "This Fixable Problem Costs U.S. Businesses $1 Trillion." Accessed June 4, 2021. https://www.gallup.com/workplace/247391/fixable-problem-costs-businesses-trillion.aspx.

Heskett, James, Thomas Jones, Gary Loveman, Earl Sasser Jr. and Leonard Schlesinger. "Putting the Service-Profit Chain to Work." *Harvard Business Review*. 1994, Republished July-August 2008. https://hbr.org/2008/07/putting-the-service-profit-chain-to-work.

Inc.com. Burkas, David. "Why the Most Successful Companies Don't Put Customers First." Accessed June 4, 2021. https://www.inc.com/david-burkus/why-the-most-successful-companies-dont-put-customers-first.html.

KnowledgeAtWharton. "Southwest Airlines' Colleen Barrett on 'Servant Leadership'." July 9, 2008. Video, 25:00. https://www.youtube.com/watch?v=6TgR95vnM0c.

Marketbridge. Hasselwander, Andy. "Customer-Centricity: Definition, Challenges, and Solutions." Accessed June 4, 2021. https://market-bridge.com/2019/10/18/customer-centricity-definition-challenges-and-solutions/.

Rykrsmith, Eva. "Your Employees Are Customers Too." *Perspectives (blog)*. October 26, 2012. https://www.quickbase.com/blog/your-employees-are-customers-too.

Rykersmith, Eva. "What is Servant Leadership? Thoughts from Southwest Airlines President, Colleen Barrett." *Perspectives (blog)*. September 20, 2010. https://www.quickbase.com/blog/what-is-servant-leadership-thoughts-from-southwest-airlines-president-colleen-barrett.

CHAPTER 7

BrainyQuote. "Treat a person as he is and he will…" Accessed October 3, 2021. https://www.brainyquote.com/quotes/jimmy_johnson_392763.

Lee Yohn, Denise. "Reminder: Customers Care How You Treat Your Employees." *Harvard Business Review*. September 26, 2018. https://hbr.org/2018/09/reminder-customers-care-how-you-treat-your-employees.

McWilliams, Abagail and Donald Siegel. "Corporate Social Responsibility: A Theory of the Firm Perspective." *Academy *of Management*, No. 26 (2001): 117–127. https://doi.org/10.5465/amr.2001.4011987.

State of the American Workplace. Washington: Gallup, 2017. https://www.gallup.com/workplace/238085/state-american-workplace-report-2017.aspx.

TEDx Talks. "How a New Lens on "HR" Can Reduce Turnover AND the Cycle of Poverty | Joe DeLoss | TEDxColumbus." December 8, 2015. Video, 11:42. https://www.youtube.com/watch?v=NxJZs7a3DWo&list=PLMJ9rvpCbsYr3A5hsw5_WpHzerVGo6lY_&index=43.

TEDx Talks. "Putting the Human Back Into Human Resources | Mary Schaefer | TEDxWilmington." September 8, 2014. Video, 9:36. https://www.youtube.com/watch?v=0Mq2TiJmqCI&list=PLMJ9rvpCbsYr3A5hsw5_WpHzerVGo6lY_&index=29.

UNIDO. "What is CSR?" United Nations Industrial Development Organization. Accessed September 10, 2021. https://www.unido.org/our-focus/advancing-economic-competitiveness/competitive-trade-capacities-and-corporate-responsibility/corporate-social-responsibility-market-integration/what-csr.

CHAPTER 8

Achievers Workforce Institute. *Achievers Engagement and Retention Report 2021*. Pleasanton: Achievers, 2021.

Association of American Chambers of Commerce in Latin America and the Caribbean. "PriceSmart." Accessed September 11, 2021. https://www.aaccla.org/leadership-circle/pricesmart/.

Binvel, Yannick, Michael Franzino, Alan Guarino, Jean-Marc Laouchez, and Werner Penk. *Future of Work: The Global Talent Crunch.* Korn Ferry, 2018.

BrainyQuote. "Colin Poawell—There are no secrets to success. It is…" Accessed October 3, 2021. https://www.brainyquote.com/quotes/colin_powell_121363?src=t_preparation.

Erb, Marcus, Nancy Cesena, Julie Musilek, and Ed Frauenheim. *Managing Millenials: 2019 Great Place to Work® Study on the Best Workplaces for Millennials.* Great Places to Work®, 2019.

Gomez, Karianne, Tiffany Mawhinney, and Kimberly Betts. *Welcome to Generation Z.* Deloitte and the Network of Executive Women, 2018.

Hamilton, Brady, Joyce Martin, and Michelle Osterman. *Vital Statistics Rapid Release: Births: Provisional Data for 2020.* Centers for Disease Control, May 2021.

Indeed. "Characteristics of "Baby Boomer" Professionals." Career Guide / Finding a Job. Accessed September 11, 2021. https://www.indeed.com/career-advice/finding-a-job/baby-boomer-characteristics.

KnowledgeAtWharton. "*Knowledge@Wharton Interview with Sherry Bahrambeygui.*" June 1, 2020. Video, 29:35. https://www.youtube.com/watch?v=FjECR_-xL4I.

Leopold, Till, Vesselina Ratcheva, and Saadia Zahidi. *The Future of Jobs Report 2018*. Cologny/Geneva: World Economic Forum, 2018.

Manpower Group. *The Great Talent Shortage Awakening: Actions to Take for a Sustainable Workforce*. Milwaukee: Manpower Group, 2013.

Manpower Group. *Talent Shortage 2020: Closing the Skills Gap: What Workers Want*. Milwaukee: Manpower Group, 2020.

Melin, Anders and Misyrlena Egkolfopoulou. "Employees Are Quitting Instead of Giving Up Working From Home." *Bloomberg Wealth,* June 1, 2021. https://www.bloomberg.com/news/articles/2021-06-01/return-to-office-employees-are-quitting-instead-of-giving-up-work-from-home.

Paychex. "How to Manage the 5 Generations in the Workplace." Human Resources | Article. Accessed June 5, 2021. https://www.paychex.com/articles/human-resources/how-to-manage-multiple-generations-in-the-workplace.

Taylor Jr., Johnny C. *Reset: A Leader's Guide to Work in an Age of Upheaval*. New York: Hachette Book Group, 2021.

Vasel, Kathryn. "Here's How the Pandemic Has Changed Work Forever." *CNN Business,* December 21, 2020. https://www.cnn.com/2020/12/21/success/job-change-remote-work-pandemic/index.html.

CHAPTER 9

Brecheisen, Jeremie. "Why HR Leaders Never Become the CEO, but Should." *Gallup.* August 29. 2019. https://www.gallup.com/workplace/265886/why-leaders-become-ceo.aspx.

Clark, Dorie. "If Strategy is So Important, Why Don't We Make Time For It?" *Harvard Business Review,* June 21, 2018. https://hbr.org/2018/06/if-strategy-is-so-important-why-dont-we-make-time-for-it.

Dumas, John. *The Mastery Journal: Master Productivity, Discipline, and Focus in 100 Days."* John Lee Dumas, 2017.

Goodreads. "Quote by Buddha: What you think you become. What you feel, you…" Accessed October 3, 2021. https://www.goodreads.com/quotes/6990654-what-you-think-you-become-what-you-feel-you-attract.

Horwath, Richard. *The Strategic Thinking Manifesto.* Strategic Thinking Institute. https://www.strategyskills.com/wp-content/uploads/The-Strategic-Thinking-Manifesto.pdf.

HRCI. "Exam Content Outlines." SPHR Exam Content Outline. Accessed September 11, 2021. https://www.hrci.org/docs/default-source/web-files/sphr-exam-content-outline.pdf?sfvrsn=7fc44f61_22.

Kabacoff, Robert. "Develop Strategic Thinkers Throughout Your Organization." *Harvard Business Review,* February 7, 2014. https://hbr.org/2014/02/develop-strategic-thinkers-throughout-your-organization.

Reimer, David and Adam Bryant. "Superhuman Resources: How HR Leaders have Redefined Their C-Suite Role." *Organizations & People*, October 28, 2020. https://www.strategy-business.com/article/Superhuman-resources-How-HR-leaders-have-redefined-their-C-suite-role.

Thinkers50. "The Thinkers50 Ranking." 2019 Thinkers50 List. Accessed September 11, 2021. https://thinkers50.com/t50-ranking/?tab=2019.

CHAPTER 10

Goodreads. "Self Improvement Quotes (3593 Quotes)." Accessed October 3, 2021. https://www.goodreads.com/quotes/tag/self-improvement.

Lowe's. "Lowe's Announces New Brand Positioning: Never Stop Improving." Lowe's. Press Release, September 19, 2011. Lowe's. Website. https://corporate.lowes.com/newsroom/press-releases/lowes-announces-new-brand-positioning-never-stop-improving-09-19-11.

Petrone, Paul. "7 Questions That Ambitious Employees Should Ask Their Boss." *LinkedIn Learning Blog*. July 29, 2019. https://www.linkedin.com/business/learning/blog/productivity-tips/questions-ambitious-employees-should-ask-their-boss.

Ratna, Abhishek. *No Parking. No Halt. Success Non-Stop.* Supernova Publishers, 2015.

CHAPTER 11

Ainomugisha, Gerald. "Management Guide to the Consultative Leadership Style." *6Q Blog*. Accessed June 5, 2021. https://inside.6q.io/consultative-leadership/.

Dinsmore Steele. "(HRO) Human Resource Outsourcing: Lifting Small Business Burdens." Learn About PEO. Accessed June 5, 2021. https://dinsmoresteele.com/dinsmore-steele-blog/hro-human-resource-outsourcing-lifting-small-business-burdens.

Forbes. "Thoughts On The Business of Life." Forbes Quotes. Accessed June 5, 2021. https://www.forbes.com/quotes/3868/.

Goodreads. "Apprach Quotes (65 quotes)." Accessed October 3, 2021. https://www.goodreads.com/quotes/tag/approach.

Harney, Rebekah. "6 Advantages of HR Outsourcing." *Resources & Insights (blog)*. May 19, 2021. https://www.lbmc.com/blog/advantages-hr-outsourcing/.

HRO Resources. "The Advantages of Outsourcing HR Functions." HRO Insights. Accessed June 5, 2021. https://hroresources.com/the-advantages-of-outsourcing-hr-functions/.

CONCLUSION

Filling The Jars. "24 Intentional Living Quotes to Inspire Your Best Life." Accessed October 3, 2021. https://www.fillingthejars.com/intentional-living-quotes/.

www.ingramcontent.com/pod-product-compliance
Lightning Source LLC
LaVergne TN
LVHW011825060526
838200LV00053B/3902